Kim Cattrall

sexualintelligence

Kim Cattrall
sexualintellig

CARLTON
BOOKS

ence

THIS IS A CARLTON BOOK

First published in Great Britain in 2005 by
Carlton Books Ltd
20 Mortimer Street
London W1T 3JW

Published by arrangement with Madison Press Books

ISBN 1 84442 296 8

A catalogue record for this book is available from the British Library

Produced by Madison Press Books
1000 Yonge Street – Suite 200
Toronto, Ontario, Canada
M4W 2K2
Printed in Singapore

6 A Note from Kim

8 Acknowledgments

10 Introduction

12 Chapter One
Desire

50 Chapter Two
Messaging

68 Chapter Three
Arousal

88 Chapter Four
Fantasy

116 Chapter Five
Release

134 Credits and Index

What ignites a personal

For me, it was a desire to define myself more clearly beyond an iconic character I played for over seven years — a character I love and fully embraced. Samantha Jones captured people's imaginations and earned a place in our collective culture.

After the first two seasons of *Sex and the City*, people began coming up to me wanting to share their own Samantha scenarios. This was flattering — but could sometimes be embarrassing as well. People assumed that I, like Samantha, had always enjoyed fabulous sex when, in fact, the opposite was true. As is the case for many women, sexual fulfillment came late. With the publication of my first book, *Satisfaction: The Art of the Female Orgasm*, I wanted to reach out to women and men with the hope that what I had eventually learned could work for them in finding their own fulfillment.

With the success of the book came a huge response from readers wanting to know more. I was approached about having my own talk show as a forum for couples. As lovely as it was to get these requests, I had to turn them down. I'm not a sex expert or a therapist.

Still, the mail and the questions continued. I could see there remained so much to explore and learn — for myself as well as everybody else! — and that's how the idea for this current investigation started. Having explored the *Satisfaction* of sexual desire, my aim now was to look at its sources and inspirations. I decided to call this new project *Sexual Intelligence* because I wanted it to be just that — a gathering of information and insights that might help increase understanding about sex.

sexual revolution?

For the next two years, working together with a small band of writers, researchers and a tiny film crew, we set out to trace and illustrate the quirky logic and impulses of desire, its sources and its rewards. Our process involved speaking to many people who could be any one of us, as well as to experts and people for whom the study of sexuality has been a life's work. We also traveled to extraordinary locations whose history in culture and art reflect a significant contribution to the story of sex in ways that continue to move us and speak to us.

This book and the companion documentary reflect our journey and celebrate all that we found. I hope you enjoy it. I feel wiser having done *Sexual Intelligence* — but the revolution continues!

— *Kim Cattrall*

Like sex,
making books and
documentaries, I've found,
is a deeply
collaborative effort.

With thanks... First and foremost, I must thank my partner
in Fertile Ground Productions — Amy Briamonte. Her inspired notions, her intellect, passion, perseverance and friendship have sustained and nurtured this endeavor in ways for which I am profoundly grateful.

Our documentary producer, Amanda Enright, provided invaluable leadership, marshaling an enormous set of elements into a solid weave both at home and abroad. The efforts of Amanda and our crew, lead by James Buchanan and Stefan von Bjorn, as well as animator Sam Javanrouh and the team at Optix Digital Pictures, are reflected in this book as well as in the documentary.

I am grateful to screenwriters Jeff Kindley, for his unerring sense of structure; Rick Green, for his unyielding sense of humor; and Amy Briamonte, for her perspicacity and the ability to keep it all together and moving forward.

The experts we interviewed extensively — Thomas Moore, Dr. Michael J. Bader, Dr. Betty Dodson and Maggie Paley — are treasured for their distinctive voices and their illuminating work. They are the beacons.

Dennis Erdman I cannot thank enough for his fierce friendship and for his unfailing capacity to stoke the flames of creativity. Nor Jennifer Gelfer, for her openhearted support — nor Kyra Panchenko and Stephen Lacey, for their talent and style.

Formidably, on the publishing side, this project flourished with the early embrace of Larry Kirschbaum of Time Warner Book Group and the ongoing, nurturing faith of Brian Soye at Madison Press Books.

I acknowledge with deepest gratitude the incredible Wanda Nowakowska, my editor at Madison. Her encouragement, heartfelt enthusiasm and civility under pressure sustained us, in more ways than can be easily expressed, throughout the formidable process of creating a documentary and a book almost simultaneously.

One of our most enormous strokes of luck came in the form of Gord Sibley, the talented designer whose inspired layouts and unstinting attention to creative detail are in evidence on every page of this book.

Thank you to Kevin Yorn, to Goodmans and to our broadcast financiers, CTV, Channel 4 and HBO.

Finally, I acknowledge with deepest admiration the seven extraordinary "ordinary" people — Antony, Cayra, Kiisti, Lisa, Natasha, Roland and Tarik — who shared with unending honesty, insight and humor their own "sexual intelligence" with us. Seekers and adventurers every one, this book is dedicated to them.

"The whole world is connected by an erotic principle. And a great deal of creative life comes out of the connections between things. I mean, it's a silly thing to say, but even putting chocolate sauce on ice cream is an erotic activity because you're putting two things together for pleasure." — Thomas Moore

"There's this myth that if you understand something like sexual arousal, you won't be able to enjoy it anymore. Just like there's an idea that understanding something replaces the poetry of it and the experience of it. I have never once found that to be true." — Michael J. Bader

Let's talk about

It's a big subject, where nature and culture collide. Sex excites our bodies, expresses our identities, feeds off our imaginations and touches our souls. It connects our deepest selves to the world outside. How we manage it determines the value it can have to enrich our lives.

But how do we navigate the mysteries of sex? We say we are swept away, possessed and overtaken — all of which acknowledge the force of desire but never its logic. Is it possible to develop a kind of sexual intelligence, one that can deepen our pleasure and give us a greater awareness of ourselves?

Chapter One
Desire

The Greek poet Sappho called desire a "delicate fire" racing beneath her skin. What better way to describe a force that draws so heavily upon both our surface and inner lives?

A constant touchstone in any exploration of desire is the connection between physicality and thoughts and feelings. What we possess physically has a bearing in some ways on what we want and how we want it — even if it's just more of the same! Whatever gender we are, or crave, it helps to make sense of the impulses *and* the equipment that go along with it.

From chemistry to physiology, men and women are tuned a bit differently. Ideally this is something to be celebrated. Tolerance, understanding and a desire to look beyond one's own experiences are key. Thomas Moore, who has written about sexuality with such sensitivity in his acclaimed book *The Soul of Sex*, told us, "We have to understand that sex is about differences coming together. Get past your narcissism where you think everyone is like you. Appreciate the other person by acknowledging their difference and their mystery." Or, as Antony, one of the people we interviewed, put it: "Well, it's just like walking into a house, eh? I mean, either you're going into the house or you're the house. It's one thing to say, 'I'm welcoming you into my house' versus a guy just saying, 'I'm going in there!'"

Lisa

Kiisti

Natasha

Antony

Roland

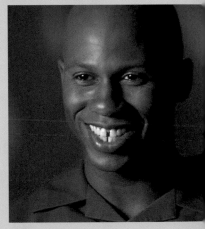

Tarik

"The most mysterious aspect of sex to me is just the male psyche in general. Men are not the most talkative of creatures and can be difficult to read sometimes." — Lisa

"All men want as much sex as they can get. I drive a nice Porsche so I can get chicks so I can have sex." — Antony

"There's still this hardcore idea of what homosexual is and what heterosexual is and what bisexual may or may not be. So I like the idea of being hetero-flexible — meaning that you're still 'hetero.'" — Kiisti

"Men can have sex any time, anywhere, any place, doesn't matter, they're up for it." — Roland

"I find that women are a lot more understanding of women not being in a sexual place at a certain time. When you're in a relationship with a man, there's a sexual frequency that's expected." — Natasha

"Even when I'm on the subway, if I've just met someone I find really cute, I wish I could have sex with that person. That urge is so powerful. It's like being ruled by your penis!" — Tarik

So many of us want simple solutions to complex problems. But they aren't always available, even when they seem to be. The little blue pill is a good example.
As a *British Medical Journal* editorial reminds us: "…just because a man's erections are improved does not mean that his sexual life at home will be."

Interestingly, with the initial success of Viagra and similar drugs, pharmaceutical companies began looking for solutions to female sexual dysfunction (FSD) — a rather vague term that encompasses everything from difficulty having orgasms to lax libidos. After eight years of research into whether Viagra could be used to treat sexual problems in women, Pfizer abandoned its trials because they proved inconclusive. Its research indicated that arousal and desire were experienced very differently by men and women.

Why didn't the little blue pill work for women? Most men take Viagra, get an erection and usually want to have sex. Women take Viagra and become lubricated but that doesn't guarantee they'll want to make love. Sexual arousal in women turns out to be far more complicated than the researchers at Pfizer thought it would be. Or maybe it's a lot simpler than they thought. Maybe they were just looking in the wrong place….

Psychology professor Roy Baumeister suggests that "women have more erotic plasticity than men." Their sex drives are shaped more by circumstances and by social and cultural forces. And physiology seems to play a smaller part in women's sexual arousal than in men's. "The *brain*," as the Pfizer scientists concluded, "is the crucial sex organ in a woman."

Many different psychological and emotional factors turn women on — or off —
according to Cynthia Graham, research scientist at the Kinsey Institute for Sex, Gender and Reproduction, Indiana University. In a 2004 study, Graham and her fellow researchers discovered that several factors enhanced or inhibited female arousal. These included feelings about one's body, concern about reputation, unwanted pregnancy, feeling desired versus feeling used by a partner, feeling accepted by a partner, how a partner approached them and negative mood. They found an "inhibitor" could be an "enhancer" in some situations. For example, the possibility of being seen or heard while having sex was arousing for some women and inhibiting for others.

Whether we're male, female or transgender, our sexual desire also fluctuates according to our age, health and social situation. Women's cycles and taking the birth control pill can have an effect too. Arousal requires sexual energy and all of us may have more energy at certain times of the day or in certain seasons. It just isn't going to happen when we're stressed out, sick, depressed, exhausted or have had too much to drink.

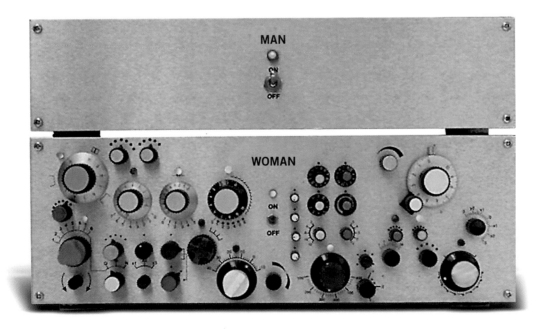

We live in a performance-driven society, so it isn't surprising that some of us worry about the ups and downs of sex. It's hard not to, when everybody on the various screens we watch is having such a good time — *all* the time.

"Normal" doesn't exist when it comes to desire and arousal. We all have our own unique body rhythms and sexual turn-ons. "A man's self-worth is wrapped up in the functioning of his penis to an inordinate degree in our culture," psychologist, sex educator and author Dr. Michael Bader told us. "The ability to achieve and maintain an erection — much less penis size — is a preoccupation for many men and accounts for the tremendous popularity of drugs like Viagra." Performance anxiety extends to women now, too. "We're meant to have orgasms like our mothers can do Sunday roasts," quipped British novelist Nikki Gemmell in a recent interview. Cathy Winks and Anne Semans (authors of *The Good Vibrations Guide to Sex*) remind us: "Perhaps the only absolute truth about sexual response is how fundamentally fluid it is. One can move from arousal to desire, from excitement to indifference, from boredom to passion, from orgasm to arousal and back again."

We can't always rely on the moans, shudders and shakes of nonverbal communication to indicate our sexual likes and dislikes. Mutually satisfying sex is built on good verbal communication. All of us have heard this over and over again, but actually talking to our partners about our needs can be difficult — in some measure because of the sexual script of our culture. "Guys are always supposed to know what to do," Kiisti, one of our interviews, told us, "but their lover's vagina requires a little learning curve. Maybe that affects their confidence. And because it affects their confidence, it's something you don't want to address."

Sexual desire fills us with the anticipation of discovering another's body and of having them discover ours.

Ideally, we want our partners to learn about our bodies and delight in what they find. In treasured moments of intimacy, powerful arousal leaves us speechless. But sometimes it can help to talk about mutual discoveries. The trouble is, many of us never do.

One reason for silence may be that we simply aren't able to find words we feel comfortable using in discussing our lover's body, or even our own. Scientific language is libido-killing, and slang can feel vulgar or foreign. In fact, some slang expressions mean one thing in one country and something quite different in another, which can lead to potentially mortifying moments. ("Fanny" in North America refers to the butt, but in Britain refers to the vulva!) Sometimes we use a word but have no idea what it actually means. Most people who call the vulva a "pussy" are thinking of something cute and kittenlike. But the slang is more likely to have come from *puss*, an Old Norse word for "purse."

The range of things that we hear and say in reference to our genitalia underscores both the enthusiasm and the fears these parts engender. Sometimes it helps just to make up our own language!

The Name Game

"Prick. Pole. Staff. Shaft."

"Yeah, Ludicrous was his name there for a while."

"Trouser Snake. Manhood. Real Deal. Main Apparatus. One-eyed Wonder."

"Johnson. Although I never understood that one!"

"The Intruder!!!"

"Hoo-hoo."

"Down there."

"The word 'vulva' is so funny. Sounds like a well-built car!"

*"When I was
growing up,
my mother
always called
it your jujube.
I kind of
like 'peach'
because it is like
a peach — and
peaches are
ripe and juicy
and nice to eat.
Peach has
a good
connotation.
'Piss clam,'
on the other
hand...Not
so sure!"* — Lisa

British researchers Virginia Braun and Celia Kitzinger conducted a follow-up to a 2001 study they had done on female genital slang. When they asked participants to match up about fifty of the most common terms for female genitalia with the part they thought it referred to, they discovered that there was very little agreement. At the top of the list of misused clinical words are "vulva" (external female genitals) and "vagina" (birth canal leading from vulva to uterus) — with "vagina" tending to take the place of "vulva" in everyday speech.

Slang's "lack of precision and consistency," say the study's authors, "makes it more difficult for women to communicate verbally with sexual partners about the location of sensations, to name what they are feeling and to explore the range of sensations possible in different locations." But do we always need words? Many women just lend a helping hand to direct their partners, or moan when the right spot has been touched. On the other hand, can women be sexually articulate if they don't have an intimate language to describe themselves?

Sexologist Dr. Betty Dodson, who has spent more than forty years helping women develop their sexual responses, understands the importance of sexual language. As she told us, "In the seventies, we used the word 'cunt' and I was happy with that. It's an old Anglo-Saxon term. And what goes with 'cunt' is 'cock.' Now, *those* are two powerful words. And when a cunt and a cock get together, well, they'll have a good time."

According to Dodson, it also helps to understand the more clinical words that describe female anatomy: "What is the vulva? It's the closest word that incorporates all the parts. Because it means 'wraparound.'" Naming the vulva has, in fact, had a long tradition. The author of the sixteenth-century book *The Perfumed Garden* obviously did a lot of hands-on research.... He named thirty-eight different types — including the Endless One, the Crested One, the Humpbacked One, the Swelling One, the Silent One....

Perhaps modern women have some catching up to do when it comes to nicknames for their private parts. Men have never lost the knack. But then again, as the old joke goes, guys don't like being bossed around by someone they don't even know!

Maggie Paley, author of the groundbreaking *The Book of the Penis*, sensitively reasons, "I think men have names for their penises because a penis is like a separate being. In fact, a man can't control it…. He doesn't always know if he's going to have an erection when he may not want one. Or if he's not going to have one when he *does* want one." Maggie ended her research and her writing with much more compassion for men. "I've always loved men," she told us, "but I have more compassion for them now than I used to."

T is for Testosterone

Male hormones play a critical role in the differences between how men and women experience desire. When Samantha Jones walks into a bar on Sports Night, looks approvingly at the wall-to-wall men and says, "I'm getting a contact high from all the testosterone," the *Sex and the City* audience knows exactly what she's talking about. Those morning hard-ons under the covers are pure testosterone uncomplicated by any conscious thought, just sweet dreams. Take away the testosterone and the erections disappear. Replace it and they reappear. It's that straightforward. (Testosterone is present in a woman's body, too, although in about one tenth the amount and with less obvious or measurable effects.)

We spoke with Griffin Hansbury, a wonderful writer and female-to-male transsexual who had been taking testosterone for two years. "I got a feminist education and I didn't really want to believe men think differently from women," he told us. "But especially when I first started with the hormones, I couldn't stop thinking about sex…. Before, I used to see women on the subway and I would have a thought process — she's attractive, I would like to get to know her — and it would be sort of a narrative. With the testosterone, the narrative was gone. I had acquired the ability to separate women into pieces — an arm, a leg, an ankle…at which I stared mindlessly…enraptured in a sort of pre-verbal daze…. It was utterly, devastatingly physical."

"*It means a lot to have an erection, that sense of pride and just revealing something with that very animalistic urge inside you. At the end, it does come down to the traditional machismo… I guess, you just feel that… alright…I'm the man!*" — Tarik

"*I like what a penis represents — the sensual, sexual, driving intensity of it. You wonder, because you don't have one, right? And it's the eternal mystery, really. If I had a penis…. Gosh, what I would do. If I had a penis for a day, the first thing I would do is have sex. And then I would pee in the snow!*" — Natasha

Given whatever management difficulties may come with having a penis, most who do have one are quick to point out that they are also a great source of joy, of power and of expression.

"I worked with Freud in Vienna.
We broke over the concept of
penis envy. Freud felt that it should
be limited to women."

— Dr. Leonard Zelig, in Woody Allen's film *Zelig*

Fabulously Phallic

Believe it or not, one way to get in touch with the power of the penis is to head for a sleepy little hamlet in Dorset, England — where the hills are as alive as you've ever seen them. There, in the high, rolling fields of grazing sheep, lies a staggering 180-foot-tall earthwork figure, plainly endowed with the largest hard-on on Earth.

Known as the Cerne Abbas Giant (but often referred to by locals simply as "the Rude Man"), the ancient outline, carved so deeply into the chalk hillside, is something of an historical mystery. The inspiration for such a staggering display of male sexual arousal fills us with wonder. The giant is believed to be almost two thousand years old and related to the Roman cult of Hercules, but no one is sure exactly why — or how — it was created so many centuries ago. Other primates try to frighten off aggressors by displaying their genitals, and perhaps that was the logic at work here (given that the figure is wielding a huge club). Historically, the site is most famous for its legendary procreative powers — and pilgrims hoping to conceive a child have long journeyed here, even into modern times.

At twenty-six feet long, the giant's endowment is more than a penis. It's a phallus.

It's not meant to be an exact...well, reproduction. It's not even *meant* for reproduction. The phallus is the myth behind the manhood. It's a work of art, a magical talisman, to be worshiped as a source of masculinity, penetrating power, fertility and life itself.

Even locals who doubt the giant is still fertile don't mind having him lay about in their backyard. They have cared for his phallus over centuries, weeding, pruning and mowing to maintain his sexy silhouette. Even the local sheep do their share. (No teeth, ladies!)

The word "phallus" comes from the Greek word *phallos*, meaning penis. Jungian analyst Eugene Monick believes that "all images through which masculinity is defined have phallos as their point of reference. Sinew, determination, effectuality, penetration, straightforwardness, hardness, strength — all have phallos giving them effect. Phallos is the fundamental mark of maleness, its stamp, its impression."

Though the Cerne Abbas Giant has the biggest phallus to survive since Roman times, it's hardly alone. Mother Nature preserved an unrivaled collection of phallic art in the ruins left by the infamous eruption of Mt. Vesuvius in 79 A.D. Back in first-century Rome, sex was openly celebrated and people believed symbolic representations of the male organ held the power to increase fertility and prosperity and to ward off evil spirits. "Good sex in whatever form was a much-appreciated gift of the gods," notes John R. Clarke, author of *Roman Sex*. "To pursue sex was a good thing — not a shameful thing. Romans stigmatized many fewer sexual practices than we do." In the open-air culture of ancient Greece and Rome, statues, paintings and carvings boasting erect penises stood proudly in courtyards and gardens or were well-hung on the walls of houses and public buildings for all to see.

Phalluses were carved into the pavement on street corners, set in bricks on the outside walls of buildings and even outfitted with little bronze bells (called *tintinnabula*) and dangled over doorways and entrance halls. Talk about having a lot of balls in the air!

Roman boys wore small coral or amber members around their necks as amulets on a necklace called a *fascinum*, which gives us the modern word "fascinating" — isn't it? "Where our culture associates any open display of male genitals with obscenity and pornography, ancient Romans regularly felt it was their *duty* to put up phallic displays where danger lurked," explains John Clarke.

Romans filled their palaces with phalluses. In the opulent House of the Vettii in Pompeii, visitors were welcomed by a fountain statue of Priapus — a son of Aphrodite and god of virility and fertility — with his penis put to good use as a waterspout. Nearby hangs a painting, still visible today, of the god weighing his huge member against a bag of coins on a scale. A man or woman of that time wouldn't think there was anything remotely offensive about these images — they were intended to protect the household and to wish its visitors prosperity and fertility.

To the Romans, the phallus was a celebration of the miracle of man, a symbol of life's cornucopia, bursting with energy and vitality. Rome built an empire on this kind of power, conquering the world with cocky confidence.

Penis power even extended to the justice system. The word "testicle" comes from the Latin *testis*, which means "to witness." Forget the hand on the heart. When the Ancients swore an oath, they cupped what they treasured most — their balls!

Hidden from View

As compelling as phallus worship was, in the Western world at least, it wouldn't last. As Rome fell, so, eventually, would the phallus. Christian theologians, particularly St. Augustine in the Middle Ages, began teaching that sexual desire was evil and that the sexual organs — especially the erect penis — were associated with the unclean, with lust and with the devil.

This spurred a centuries-long campaign to fell the forest of phalluses left behind by pagan culture. Never again in the history of Western art would the inspiration of the penis be acknowledged quite so literally — or given so much…weight.

Back in Dorset, they filled in (for a time) the ditches that made up the Cerne Abbas Giant's penis. All over Europe, statues lost their marbles, castings were castrated and some paintings got a second coat. The phallus had become taboo — outdone by a strategically placed fig leaf.

In the eighteenth and nineteenth centuries, during excavations at the ancient site of the buried city of Pompeii, archaeologists uncovered artifacts that were remarkably preserved and — to their sensibilities — remarkably perverted. Phallic art and representations of Roman sexuality that had been hidden for almost two thousand years would soon be hidden from view again, but this time by Royal decree.

In 1819, the King of Naples unwittingly brought his daughter along to tour artifacts excavated from sites in Pompeii. What he saw shocked and embarrassed him and he ordered that a room be set aside in the National Archaeological Museum of Naples for all offending wall paintings and objects. What was once publicly celebrated became a peep show feeding into the deep vein of eroticism surrounding all things forbidden. The Cabinet of Obscene Objects — or "secret museum," as it came to be known — has been inaccessible to all but a few for much of its history.

The term "pornography," in fact, was first coined by a German scholar in 1850 in reference to art catalogs containing sketches of artifacts from Pompeii. He combined the Greek words *porne* ("whore") and *graphein* ("to write") to form "pornography." The word caught on. So, I suppose, did the concept.

Fear of the phallus continues to the present day. An erect penis, or even one that is not erect, is generally suitable only for private viewing. Phallic symbols, on the other hand, have become part of the social landscape — hiding in plain sight as skyscrapers, rockets, racecars, cigars and neckties.

Maggie Paley made a fascinating point to us on the matter: "Certainly during the twentieth century, there was very little that we could see of penis representation in art. This is the power of non-disclosure.

The woman is out there for everyone to see but the man is hidden behind his pants.

It's a great, a powerful, position — but it leaves the man unknown. I think true power comes from communication and disclosure. There are men who feel they'll lose power that way. But in fact you don't lose power by disclosing secrets, because the power is in the mystery. And the mystery is always going to be there."

Happily, the National Archaeological Museum of Naples completely refurbished the "secret museum" in a stunning renovation and opened its doors to the public in 2000. It's a remarkable place to visit, and touring it was an unforgettable experience.

The Secret Museum

Erotic wall murals, such as the ones above depicting couples in various sex acts, are among the many sexually explicit Roman artifacts now on public display in the Gabinetto Segreto, or "secret museum," at the National Archaeological Museum of Naples. The Archaeological Museum itself houses one of the world's largest and most important collections of material culture from the classical world — including archaeological treasures from the nearby buried cities of Herculaneum and Pompeii. Inside the secret museum, a spectacular display of paintings, statuary, wall hangings and other ornaments celebrates the pleasure-seeking lifestyle the Romans clearly enjoyed — and claimed as their right.

Ironically, back when huge phalluses were worshiped, Greeks and Romans preferred dainty penises on humans.

Big sex organs were considered vulgar, ugly and coarse — a physical sign that a man was likely to be oversexed, greedy and unreliable. Hmmmmm…

Judging by all the penis enlargement ads we're bombarded with in daily e-mails, the small penis ideal does not seem to have endured. Could it be that without giant phalluses around to admire, the big job of promoting penis power has fallen to the organ itself?

Bernie Zilbergeld, author of *The New Male Sexuality*, makes a telling point: "Penises in fantasyland come in only three sizes: large, extra large and so big you can't get them through the door." Our society is obsessed with large sexual parts. Penises on men, breasts and butts on women. Some enthusiasts even play a guessing game. They claim they can tell the size of a man's penis by the shape and size of his thumb or by the length of his nose. Researchers, however, maintain that it's the index finger measured from the thumb crease to the tip that indicates the penis's flaccid length.

The naked truth? The average erect penis is about six inches long regardless of the length of the penis at rest or the size of a man's body — or any other part of his anatomy. It's the reason William H. Masters and Virginia E. Johnson, the famous sex physiologists of the 1960s, called erection the "great equalizer."

In her practice, Betty Dodson is often asked, "Am I normal?" Her reply? "The guys in the porn movies are hired for the size of their dicks. So a man walking around with a perfectly good five-and-a-half-inch dick thinks there's something wrong with his because he doesn't have an eight-inch schlong like Harry in the movie…. Women do the same thing now. They're coming to me and saying, 'I think my clit's too small.' There's an enormous amount of pressure in the culture on how we're supposed to look."

Thousands of men in the United States and elsewhere have undergone surgery to increase the size of their penises. According to Nancy Etcoff in *Survival of the Prettiest*, of three hundred men asked by a physician why they were interested in penile enhancement, only a third said it was due to complaints from female partners. "The majority expressed what is now

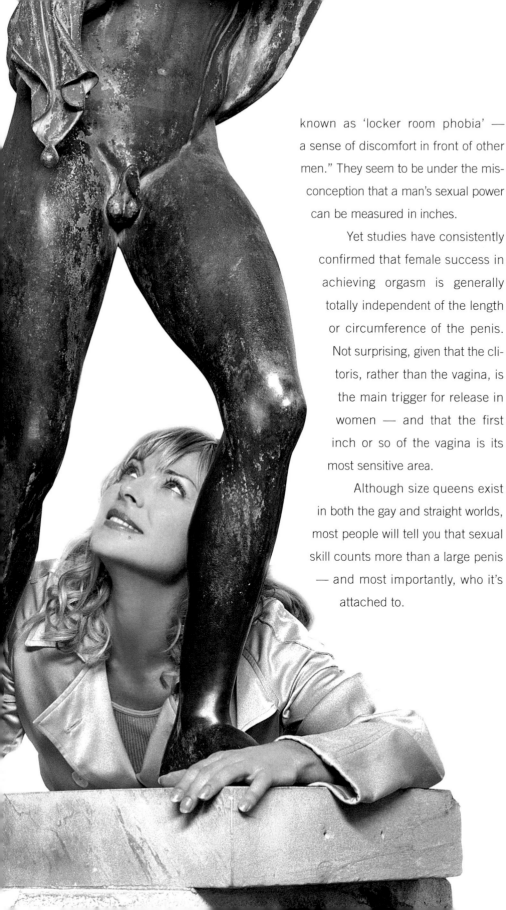

known as 'locker room phobia' — a sense of discomfort in front of other men." They seem to be under the misconception that a man's sexual power can be measured in inches.

Yet studies have consistently confirmed that female success in achieving orgasm is generally totally independent of the length or circumference of the penis. Not surprising, given that the clitoris, rather than the vagina, is the main trigger for release in women — and that the first inch or so of the vagina is its most sensitive area.

Although size queens exist in both the gay and straight worlds, most people will tell you that sexual skill counts more than a large penis — and most importantly, who it's attached to.

"Most men are definitely very consumed with how their penises look, the size, the shape. But some people are way too obsessed about it. I've been with men who actually ask me to give them feedback about their penises. We have to focus on their penis and that's a turn-off." — Tarik

"I tend to lean toward bigger penises rather than smaller ones, just because they're more penile to me. Pushing up against fabric. Pants, jeans, tighty-whities. Love the bulge!" — Natasha

"Size and shape are definitely important within certain measurements. If you're too big, ouch, it's just too much for me to work with!" — Lisa

"I think, if you asked around, I think girth is a very important element. It has to fit. If it doesn't, if it's too long, it's not fun necessarily." — Kiisti

"Most men are about the same." — Antony

The VULVA

If the penis has been subjected to a "quantity equals quality" mentality, the vulva — with its hidden physiology and puzzling architecture — has managed to at least retain a bit of mystery. Yet, for much of human history, "mysteries" surrounding the female form have not necessarily worked in women's favor. Thankfully, the sexual revolution of the 1960s has caused much more to be said — and much more to be learned — about the female anatomy. In fact, if the phallus was banished and then vanished from view, the female form is doing quite the opposite. But then, it *is* quite the opposite. These days, the vulva is out and about and the talk of the town!

"I think it's very positive that women are learning about their vaginas," sex therapist Wendy Maltz says. "When you're the best expert and authority on your own sexuality, then you're in power."

Betty Dodson couldn't agree more: "I think it's important for women to look at their sex organs so that they know what they have and to learn that, whatever the shape or form, it has its own beauty...."

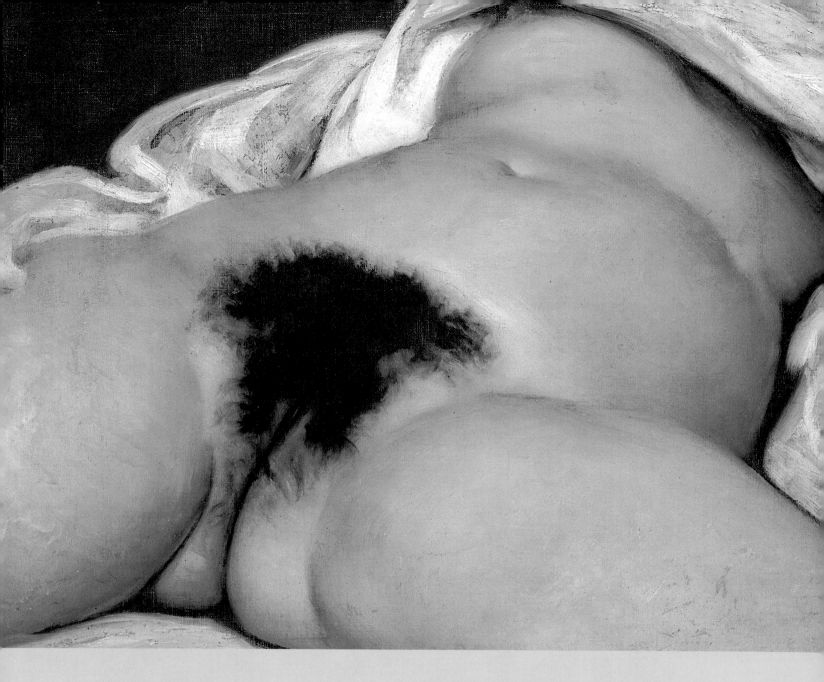

An analogy I use is, 'How would you like to go through life and never have an image of your face?' It doesn't make sense to me, not knowing what the source of your pleasure looks like."

The vulva has not always been under wraps. About 30,000 B.C., people believed the vulva to be the sole source of life. Its image was carved into stone as a kind of gateway to God. But that position didn't last long. Once humankind figured out that men also played a role in baby-making, the penis began its enduring ascension as an object of worship and men were catapulted into a role of social dominance. "Whatever the marital custom before that time — monogamy, polygyny, polyandry — after it, women's sexual freedom began to be seriously curtailed," writes Reay Tannahill in *Sex in History*.

By the nineteenth century, a woman of the upper classes in Europe wouldn't think of looking at herself naked in a mirror. Her maid would sprinkle a special powder on her *jeune fille*'s bath to cloud the water, preventing her employer from catching even the slightest glimpse of herself.

Out of her bath and dressed, a woman wore more clothing between 1830 and 1914 than at any other time in history.

In her seminal book on fashion and art, *Seeing through Clothes*, Anne Hollander talks about "the divided monster" in discussing women's fashions throughout most of European history: "Women followed a pattern of extreme exposure for the whole upper body, accompanied by ever more extreme upholstery and drapery for the lower half. The trend continued to evolve into the twentieth century, until sleeves were done away with altogether and women's bodies were exposed from the tip of their heads to their armpits while their lower half seemed to exist in its own entire universe of fabric."

The Mermaid Myth

The strapless evening gown, which remains extremely popular for romantic or "black tie" events, corresponds, Anne Hollander tells us, "to a very tenacious myth about women, the same one that gave rise to the image of the mermaid — the perniciously divided female monster.... Her face, voice, bosom and hair, her neck and arms are all entrancing, all that suggests the unreserved, tender and physically delicious love of mothers, even when it seems to promise the rough strife of adult sex. The upper half of a woman offers both keen pleasure and the illusion of sweet safety — but it is a trap. Below, under the foam, the swirling waves of lovely skirt, her hidden body repels its shapeliness armed in scaly refusal, its oceanic interior stinking of uncleanness."

Hollander points out that, for modern women, "a necessary move in the theater of sexual politics was the articulation of a woman's whole body — showing, in pants and short skirts, that women have working legs, livers and spleens just as men do. And, by extension, brains."

The word "pudendum," used to describe the external anatomy of a woman, comes from the Latin *pudere* (to be ashamed). But Mother Nature has never shied away from putting the pudendum front and center.

The female form can be found in seedpods, seashells, caves and crevices — even in the undulations of stone.

Flowers, with their soft folds and deep recesses, have also had a long symbolic association with the vulva. The lotus, for example, was viewed by mystics as the Goddess's gate, and sex was the way through the gate to her inner mysteries.

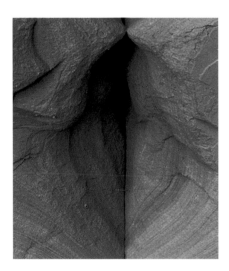

"The doorway is a kind of 'vulva' image. In earlier ages, people made a great deal of doorways.... To go from the ordinary world to an interior life, to go inward, to go inside a place — especially a place that might have a bit of mystery to it — is, I think, one of these 'vulva' experiences." — Thomas Moore

(Opposite) The inner chamber of the cave of the Sibyl, at Cumae, Italy. Sibyls were ecstatic female prophetesses who delivered oracles. Michelangelo depicted the Cumaean Sibyl in the Sistine Chapel, as she was believed to have foretold the coming of Christ.

The legendary romantic poem *Tristan and Isolde* expresses the mysteries of the vulva in its references to the "grotto of love." That's where the lovers have the opportunity to fulfill their sexual desires without interference. The poet, Gottfried von Strassburg, emphasizes the remoteness of the cave from civilization. The lovers must travel for two days before reaching it in a wild forest. It is a primeval cave — a natural, hidden enclosure — totally removed from the lovers' Christian world and all its strictures.

Art lovers have always considered Georgia O'Keeffe's paintings "gloriously female," in the words of one art critic in 1921 — even though the artist herself was uncomfortable with such descriptions. "When people read erotic symbols into my paintings, they're really talking about their own affairs," she would sniff. (Asked once why she painted oversized flowers, O'Keeffe explained that they simply provided a refuge from the ugliness of a New York winter.)

When the Whitney Museum held a retrospective of O'Keeffe's work in 1970, a new generation of sexually liberated women was introduced to her paintings. These young women embraced the sexual symbolism they saw in the bold florals. One woman who drew inspiration from O'Keeffe's work was artist Judy Chicago. Her 1979 art installation *The Dinner Party* portrayed a triangular table set for thirty-nine important women in history. She sculpted each china plate with the swirling shapes of butterflies, flowers and female genitalia. Georgia O'Keeffe, who died in 1986, was the only living woman included in the piece. Today, images of the vulva make ever-bolder appearances, moving beyond artistic metaphor

and into more literal, sometimes playful, incarnations in instructional videos, coloring books and even hand puppets.

In the seventies, Betty Dodson self-published a book called *Liberating Masturbation*, including in it pen-and-ink drawings of her friends' vulvas. "I sold 150,000 copies and carted them off to the post office in a shopping cart," Dodson told us. "I called it the orgasm express. Every time I mailed out a book, I thought, 'I'm mailing out an orgasm.'"

Dodson, who pioneered a masturbation workshop to help women learn how to reach orgasm with clitoral stimulation, encourages her clients to take a look for themselves. "I always say, 'Have you examined your genitals in a good light with the mirror?' And they tell me, 'Oh yeah, yeah.' But it turns out that they've been in the bathroom, they've lifted up

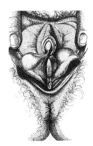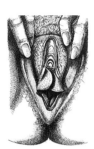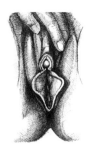

a leg and they've held a mirror down and they've pulled [the vulva] open to one side and they're looking for a pimple or a bump or to see if there's something wrong. So it isn't like sitting back and, you know, framing it, getting a good light, opening it with both hands, looking and finding out what the different parts are. And appreciating it."

In Dodson's groundbreaking instructional video, *Viva La Vulva*, we see her encourage women to look at their vulvas in the mirror and share in the amazing individual diversity and beauty to be found there. We and so many others found viewing this video to be a watershed event in shaping our appreciation and understanding of what each one of us possesses between our legs.

Since September 2000, New York photographer Alexandra Jacoby has been capturing glimpses of women's most private parts — documenting the endless variety of unscripted, unretouched vulvas. When Jacoby first started photographing the "average [vulva]," she quickly realized that there is no such thing. According to Jacoby, "each is strikingly unique, and most of us never have the opportunity to see just how personal and powerful this part of the body actually is."

During the course of our research, we discovered that people's *reactions* to looking at the vulva can be almost as varied as the vulvas themselves:

"When I looked at my own vagina in a mirror...it was actually when I was trying to get pregnant. So, it was about two years ago. And, you know, I had never looked at it. And it was very, very beautiful. It just encompasses all that's female." — Cayra

"Looks awful, feels great." — Antony

"My analogy is, it's like a newborn. Everybody thinks that a newborn, when they first come out of the womb, 'Oh, they're cute' and 'Look at the baby, it's so cute.' I'm like, are you kidding me, are we seeing the same thing? That baby's ugly!" — Roland

"I think my labia minora is too long. One of the lips is longer than the other one and it tends to kind of peek out a little bit and that bothers me a little." — Natasha

Betty Dodson talked to us about what she feels is a regrettable trend: "[Take] porn movies now…. If women have long, flowing, beautiful, Renaissance inner lips — which are one of my favorites — they go and get them cut off so they look like, you know, little clean symmetrical lines. So everybody has this sort of image of what they think a pussy is supposed to look like, I guess. We do it with our faces, don't we? We change our noses, we get cosmetic surgery, we can never get the right hairdo…. So the same thing goes on [with genitalia]."

Despite a willingness to bare all, the vulva still retains an amazing amount of mystery. And the G-Spot is one of the most controversial. In 1944, gynecologist Dr. Ernst Gräfenberg boldly went where millions of men had gone before to name it and claim it. And it's anatomical — identified by a tiny cluster of prostate-like tissue also known as a paraurethral sponge (it feels a lot better than it sounds!). Up the hill and around the bend of our vaginal canals is the sweet spot where a little touch goes a very long way….

But the G-Spot doesn't even come close to the vulva's most unique treasure — the clitoris. It's a miracle. The only organ designed strictly for pleasure. The animal kingdom is not exactly kingdom come…. In fact, humans may be the only species in which females have an orgasm — with special thanks to the little lady in the canoe.

The Secret Life of the Clitoris

Located below the pubic bone, within and close to the top of the labia, the clitoral glans — Clit, Head, Bean, Acorn, Chickpea — is simply a bundle of nerves. "Eight *thousand* nerve fibers, to be precise," writes Natalie Angier in *Woman: An Intimate Geography*. "That's a higher concentration of nerve fibers than is found anywhere else in the body, including the fingertips, lips and tongue. And it's twice — *twice* — the number found in the penis." (As Angier tellingly quips: "Who needs a handgun when you've got a semiautomatic?")

The inner lips, or labia minora, enclose the glans, the vaginal opening and the urethral opening. Beneath these structures are the invisible parts that, together, make the clitoris as large as the average penis. (In other words, women have about as much erectile tissue as men do.) The clitoral shaft runs from the glans for about an inch toward the pubic mound and then bends and divides down either side of the vaginal opening under the lips.

During arousal, the shaft fills with blood and is extremely sensitive. Two bulbs of erectile tissue also run under the inner lips and become erect when aroused. The erectile tissue surrounding the two-inch-long urethra is the paraurethral sponge. When filled with blood, the G-Spot on the sponge can be felt by pressing up through the vaginal wall toward the pubic mound. Together, these invisible structures make up what has been called the "powerhouse of orgasm."

Even for the well-initiated, getting to know the female anatomy has a certain learning curve. And where there's learning, there can be fear of failure.

As Michael Bader tells us, "Being able to enter the vagina represents being important enough — appealing enough and powerful enough — to gain entry to some place that is special. At the same time, the vagina can represent in a man's mind a place where he can be swallowed up, he can be rendered impotent. And sometimes that's too much for him to deal with."

I say, practice makes perfect. And whatever we can do to prepare ourselves and each other for greater understanding is a service. Betty Dodson took a stand on that point by telling us, "When we're kids growing up, the mommy says, 'Little Billy has a penis and little Mary has a vagina. And when Billy puts his penis inside Mary's vagina, that's how a baby is made.' And what we *should* be saying is, 'Little Billy has a penis and little Mary has a clitoris. And when they touch them in a special way, it feels good.' Well, we're a long way off from that message."

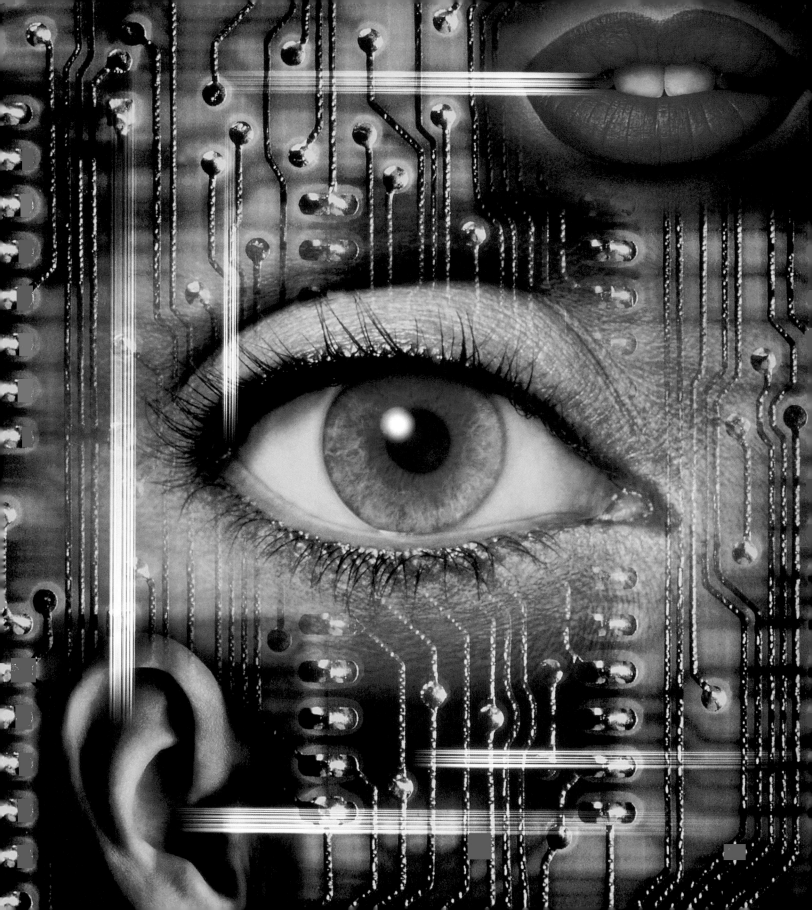

Chapter Two
Messaging

There's one organ that outdoes them all when it comes to sexual arousal and that's the brain. As the processor of stimulation, the target of hormonal mood chemicals *and* the seat of our imaginations, emotions and individual identities, the brain is by far the most powerful erogenous zone. "Sexual pleasure occurs in the brain, not in the genitals or in the peripheral nervous system," Michael Bader explained to us. "Those are simply pleasure receptors and nerve endings. You can touch them and feel no pleasure at all. Or you can touch them and feel a great deal of pleasure. The difference is the context and the meaning."

Psychologists Paul Abramson and Steven Pinkerton underscore the point: "When an erogenous zone is stimulated, the signals received by the brain are not inherently pleasurable — or even inherently sexual. Our minds need to interpret the signals. It is this interpretive stage that admits the profound influences of culture and context in the experience of sexual pleasure."

> *"Sex can be so many things. It can be everything, and it can be nothing. Sex is in your head. Yes, we have the hardware, but to be sexually engaged, I guess for myself, this [pointing to her head] has to be working. Because if this isn't working, then this [pointing down below] isn't working at all."* — Kiisti

Eye Talk In *Love in the Time of Cholera*, Gabriel García Márquez describes two lovers seeing each other for the first time: "...the girl raised her eyes to see who was passing by the window, and that casual glance was the beginning of a cataclysm of love that still had not ended half a century later." But how *do* we get from glance to cataclysm of love?

Nancy Etcoff, author of *Survival of the Prettiest*, tells us that it takes only a fraction of a second to not only recognize — but also rate — how alluring someone is. What's even more remarkable, according to researchers, is that our opinions tend to hold firm even when we're given a longer look. When it comes to sex appeal, it seems that first impressions are, indeed, lasting.

The gaze is a distinguishing courting ploy for both humans and primates, writes Helen Fisher in *Anatomy of Love*. People will often stare at their lovers for several seconds, pupils dilating all the while, before they look away. She notes that the custom of women wearing veils as a measure of chastity actually elevates this powerful language of seduction to a high art. Eye contact, Fisher tells us, "triggers a primitive part of our brain that stimulates one of two basic emotions — approach or retreat."

Perhaps because men's success in lovemaking is "performance-driven," the male gaze is keenly tied to a sensitive network of receptors governing physiological responses.

When men like what they see, hormone stimulators released on the brain can make it difficult for them to re-focus their attention anywhere else. (Well, that could help explain a lot!)

The visual stimulation that triggers involuntary, seemingly "magical," physiological responses makes men more susceptible to — but not alone in — pursuing fetishistic sexual behavior. They are more likely to rely on attributes, even objects, that they know for sure will successfully initiate arousal. Psychiatrist Dr. Robert J. Stoller, internationally renowned for his groundbreaking work on sex and gender, has described "most men of most cultures as a whole race of erotic mini-fetishists." Men talk about being a "leg man" or "a breast man" and many can go into extraordinary detail about what body part they like best.

Reveal it? Or Conceal it?

In *The Soul of Sex*, Thomas Moore reminds us that we cannot separate our bodies from our imagination: "We are always living in a story, always surrounded by images and always perceiving with imagination." One of the most potent ways in which our bodies and imaginations comment on each other is in the interplay of what we choose to cover — and what remains bare.

Clothing and fashion have, from the very first, played with peek-a-boo themes and the allure of conceal and reveal.

Wealthy women in Ancient Egypt were famously beguiling, sashaying beneath wildly expensive shifts of translucent, deeply pleated gauze that barely covered but ceaselessly caressed their naked, or partially naked, bodies. And what are fig leaves if not signposts saying, "Here it is!" Their color and shape serve to draw the eye — and add mystery — to an otherwise fully nude figure. As do bikinis and lingerie today.

The display of "genital maps" comes to us straight from the animal kingdom, where it is used to purposeful effect. Bonobo monkeys (our closest genetic relative) have in their reproductive arsenal an impressive battery of effects to heighten the appearance of their sexual viability. Throughout the animal kingdom, genital mappings may transpose genital images to the head, face or other parts of the body. We use our clothing in much the same way — cinching, tucking, padding or pleating to accentuate our sexiest parts.

The varied traditional societies of Africa, for example — where adornment and clothing are generally minimal — infuse courtship rituals with a riot of color. In the transporting book *African Ceremonies*, photographers Carol Beckwith and Angela Fisher document stunning examples of ritualized body decoration associated with coupling and allure.

Included are the Wodaabe, who reside in Central Niger between the Sahara and the grasslands. The men undergo ornate preparations for love rituals by applying pale yellow powder to lighten their faces, outlining their eyes with black kohl to heighten the whiteness of teeth and eyes, and painting a line from forehead to chin to elongate the nose. This highly codified language of ornamentation in Wodaabe men speaks to the universal impulse to adorn oneself carefully in preparation for love and for the contest of allure.

(Opposite) The diaphanous, deeply pleated fabric favored by Egyptian women of stature and wealth is evident in this finely carved fragment, thought to be Nefertiti. (Left) Sophia Loren takes the allure of "conceal and reveal" to seductive extremes. (Right) Beckwith and Fisher photographed these young Dinka herders dressed in beaded corsets that accentuate the body's allure.

Do You Have a Do?

Whether sensually tossed, tightly trussed, shaved, shorn, "twisted, beaded, braided / powdered, flowered / bangled, tangled, spangled or spaghettied" (to almost quote the song), hair works a special magic. In the realm of allure, it's a serious signifier — the place on our bodies where nature and culture literally collide. And as such, hair commands tremendous attention in life, art and sex. From New York to Tokyo, special salons carry on traditions where hair is woven, molded and sculpted in a codified mythology of sensuality and innuendo. In fact, some hair ornamentation is so intricate and studied that it has crossed over into the realm of art — for example, the suggestively female "split peach" imagery revealed in the hairdo of every geisha when her back is turned.

History has shown an enduring love affair with long, flowing hair. As Anne Hollander points out in *Sex and Suits*, it evokes freedom and sexual viability — both traditionally granted more easily to men than to women. From the mythic gods and Renaissance princes to rock stars, long hair on men was, and is, a sign of freedom and virility. The long hair of women, on the other hand, was braided, curled, pinned or knotted up and interwoven with trimmings to keep the tactile sensuality of it acceptably under wraps.

Mary Magdalene, Hollander tells us, is always depicted with tumultuous tresses that issued "an overt sexual invitation. Her hair was a potent female attribute not to be displayed in public. On the other hand, respectable unmarried girls — just like the Virgin Mary — have worn loose hair to suggest the power of female chastity. To the approving eye, their desire is unawakened, like that of children, and their cloak of hair is a pure gift from God."

According to Hollander, "This is still the case in current fashion, another sign of reliance on ancient themes. Unawakened desire in a full-grown girl is a powerful asset. Queen Elizabeth I wore loose hair at her coronation, along with pounds of jewels and brocade, to advertise her virgin status as part of her power, both sexual and temporal."

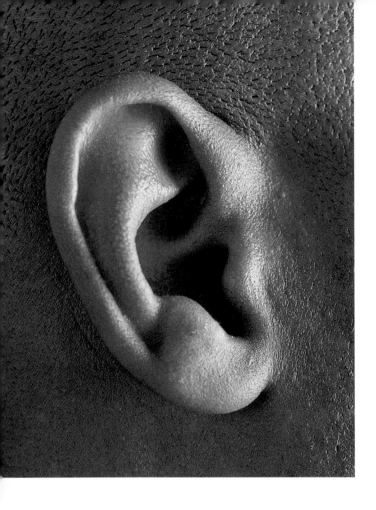

Listen… It's been said that the music we listen to during the time of our sexual awakening becomes the music we want to hear our whole lives. And it's true that our ears occupy a powerful position in the landscape of arousal. Even sweet nothings become quite something when whispered there. Though fully exposed, our ears are experienced more as private parts than as part of the face we present to the world. Seldom do we touch another's ear. But when we do, a kiss or caress on the ear is an absolutely swoon-producing gesture of tenderness.

Music… breathing… a lover's moan or smiling sigh…
Each transports us out of ordinary time
and into a realm that is deeply personal and intimate.

In *Adam's Navel*, a wonderful investigation into the cultural history of the body, author Michael Sims reminds us that "once upon a time, the female ear was considered a near-obscene imitation of the female genitals — its coil slyly imitating the labia, its channel dangerously reminiscent of a different orifice." And he points out that the idea is supported by ancient mythology, where birth from the ear is not uncommon. "Spiraling, folded inward, both the ear and the shell seemed visually reminiscent of the vulva — and therefore symbolic of both sexual intercourse and birth."

Cupid's Dart

The Ancient Greeks wrote about the god Eros — as in "erotic." Today, we all know him as Cupid, the cute little guy with the arrows who's featured on Valentine cards. But before greeting card companies turned Eros into a chubby, cherubic chocolate pusher, people were more in touch with the guy's power. He's the god of carnal desire. When the Greeks dreamed him up, those little poison darts were state-of-the-art weaponry, capable of inflicting mortal wounds of love.

The most up-to-date scientific research tells us that natural amphetamines and MAO (monoamine oxidase) inhibitors, acting as antidepressants, are the addictive potion on Cupid's darts that make our hearts pound, our faces flush and our tongues tangle. Add some euphoria, and it's definitely a transporting ride. "Getting high from the brain chemistries

of love may one day explain why some people are love junkies who ride the wave of one love affair to the next," believes seminal sexologist Dr. John Money. But even the highs of a full-blown love affair eventually change and fade. Why is that?

In his highly amusing and massively researched book *Sexy Origins and Intimate Things*, master sleuth Charles Panati tells us that the painkilling, morphine-like hormones released on our brains during the early stages of love — the ones that make us feel "drugged" by our lovers — last for only two to three years before we build up a tolerance for them and the secretions start to wane. He points out that divorce rates peak around the fourth year of marriage, just after the initial highs of love have lost their chemical underpinnings. The film *The Seven Year Itch* might better reflect scientific research, he suggests, if it were called the "four-year itch that took seven years to scratch!"

Given such dramatic findings, one wonders (if only in the interest of self-preservation) exactly *how* these potent hormones and chemicals — that have such pivotal roles in our sex lives — are brought into play. By other chemicals, of course. It appears that while we are taking in the big picture of our partner, we are also sampling them on a molecular level. The right combination of macro and micro sexual signals fills us with expectation and sets us on a wave of raw desire.

Sending and Receiving

There are many ways we send and receive sexual signals. Think of the person who licks his lips or touches her hair while talking to someone new. Or those who cross and uncross their arms and pull back their shoulders to emphasize breasts or pecs. Then there are the less obvious sexual signals. Although we seem to use our eyes more than our noses in the dating game, new research into the complex network that governs our sense of smell may one day lead to an understanding of how smells influence our sexual behavior. Researchers long ago discovered that airborne molecules called pheromones — from the Greek words *pherein*, "to transfer," and *hormon*, "to excite" — influence the choice of partners in other species and may play a role in human sexual attraction as well.

Perfume shares a long history with sexual desire. For generations, people have known that fragrance moves emotion.

The *Kama Sutra* recommends saffron, musk and sandalwood as "substances whose smell blends with that of the woman and encourages sexual excitation." Even the Bible contributes to the literature on fragrance and desire, in Proverbs 7:17–18: "I have perfumed my bed with myrrh, aloes and cinnamon. Come, let us take our fill of love until the morning; let us solace ourselves with loves."

We each exude our own unique scents and, natural or perfumed, they become part of our sexual persona. Some scents even carry memories of our first sexual awakenings. Lisa, one of our interviews, recalls being in a boutique "and the guy behind the counter smelled great. The scent aroused something in me, a memory. I asked him what he was wearing and it was Drakkar Noir, for heaven's sake, which was popular when I was in high school."

Tristram Wyatt, author of *Pheromones and Animal Behaviour*, reports that "the most searched-for human smell is a releaser pheromone that will make the wearer irresistible to potential partners."

Breathe Deep

When researchers at the Smell and Taste Treatment and Research Foundation in Chicago conducted a study on the effects, if any, of fragrances on male sexual arousal, they used floral scents and threw in the smell of baked cinnamon buns as a control. As each group smelled each test scent, individual blood flow in men's penises was measured using a small blood-pressure cuff, called a phallometer, attached to the penis. To the researchers' surprise, the sticky buns raised their subjects' blood flow more than any other scent.

In a follow-up study, the clear arousal winner proved to be a combination of lavender and pumpkin pie spices (cinnamon, nutmeg and ginger) — followed by the cinnamon buns again, a combination of licorice and doughnuts, pumpkin pie and doughnuts, buttered popcorn, orange scent and musk. Lavender, which is an old-fashioned aphrodisiac, scored the highest with the most sexually active volunteers, while strawberry topped the charts for men who reported the most satisfaction with their sex lives. As for the losing scents — cranberry, chocolate and baby powder (are we surprised?) bottomed out.

No one knows why the test subjects had these responses to these particular odors. Dr. Alan R. Hirsch, author of Scentsational Sex: The Secret to Using Aroma for Arousal, *speculates that food odors may put men in a good mood, while lavender is known to reduce anxiety. And it may be that our brains are still wired to link times of plentiful food with an increased opportunity for sex.*

Several companies already sell pheromone-based perfume additives as sexual attractants. However, it's a controversial claim. Despite how appealing the idea of the irresistible smell is, and the many products marketed on the strength of it, "there is no good evidence yet that any smell will guarantee — or even increase — success," writes Wyatt.

Since it appears that pheromones are most effective when they're your own and that lovely perfumes can leave behind a potent sense memory, the prescription is simple. Pick a perfume or cologne based on what pleases your nose, make sure it blends with the smell of your own skin and don't use so much that it covers up what you've already got going for you!

Interestingly, a steroid discovered in the naturally musky scent of men is also found in black truffles — those delectable, incredibly expensive French fungi. Jean Anthelme Brillat-Savarin, the nineteenth-century French food expert, wrote that the delicate aroma and taste of truffles could "make women more affectionate and men more attentive." Which brings us to aphrodisiacs — named, of course, after the Greek goddess of sex, Aphrodite.

Aphrodite's Appetite

Aphrodite (who, by the way, is Cupid's mother) lives on in our language as the root for "aphrodisiac" — foods that pique amorous desire. The wonderful South American novelist and cook Isabel Allende writes in *Aphrodite: A Memoir of the Senses*: "Appetite and sex are the great motivators of history. They preserve and propagate the species; they provoke wars and songs; they influence religions, law and art. All of creation is one long, uninterrupted cycle of digestion and fertility."

The foods we eat can affect the chemicals in our brains and regulate our moods: carbohydrates act like a natural tranquilizer, while protein increases energy and alertness levels. But what about our libidos? Are there foods that can turn us on?

Our ancestors certainly believed there were. Some imaginative matchmakers from long ago intuited that if a food looked like a sexual organ, it must have sexual powers. Ginseng, or "man root," played an important role in traditional Chinese and Native American love potions. Ancient Egyptians and Greeks favored mandrake, with its penis-like root. In Europe, the very erect-looking horseradish was thought to restore sexual vigor after intercourse. And, apparently, the more thick and juicy asparagus spears you ate, the more lovers you could entice into your bed.

Ancient love charms and drinks also included manly looking roots as well as numerous fruits, herbs and spices. While people today have been known to enjoy nibbling on strategically placed pineapple rings, women in days gone by were instructed to serve the juicy fruit to their lovers sprinkled with chili powder to enhance its aphrodisiac qualities.

The pomegranate's reddish-pink flowers symbolized the vulva — and its liquid, the blood of Dionysus, Aphrodite's sensual, fun-loving consort. Erotic recipes frequently called for dashes of ginger, nutmeg, cloves, cinnamon, cardamom or pepper to spice things up.

Aphrodite means "sea foam," and the goddess is deeply associated with the sea. Perhaps that's why the most famous aphrodisiacs have come from the ocean. Seashells — jewellike enclosures protecting a salty-sweet food — have always been associated with erotic allure.

Oysters, cockles, scallops, mussels, periwinkles and conch... "Since antiquity, shells...have been reputed to incite the flames of love," writes Christian Rätsch in *Plants of Love*.

"The flesh of shells and snails was consumed as an aphrodisiac meal, while the shells themselves, which so clearly recall the female form, were fashioned into magical amulets and powerful love charms."

Science has never found evidence that any food considered an aphrodisiac actually works on our brain chemistry to increase sexual desire. But we still keep feeding our lovers chocolate, oysters and champagne. And why not? The authors of *Understanding Human Sexuality* suggest that "some substances gain a continued reputation as aphrodisiacs because simply believing that something will be arousing can itself be arousing. The belief that a bull's testicles ('prairie oysters') or peanuts or clams have special powers may produce a temporary improvement of sexual functioning — not because of the chemicals contained in them but because of a *belief* in them."

I suppose these out-of-the-ordinary foods play into a mood of risk, daring and special-occasion that sparks our expectations, feeds our imaginations and heightens our senses — all of which are good for sex. Still, while I love oysters, chocolate and champagne, I take my cue from Betty Dodson, who reminds us that "the best aphrodisiac is a healthy body and an open mind."

Chapter Three
Arousal

Thanks to the near-miraculous tracking of molecules, scientists now understand something of the complex chemical processes by which pleasure and arousal are delivered into, and drained from, the bloodstream. But what makes Cupid reach into his quiver in the first place?

While the firing systems for arousal are powerful, the psychology is both subtle and complex. As Michael Bader tells us, "We think that our sexual energy and our libidos are so natural and so powerful they'll just break through any restraint: 'Just give me half a chance and I'm raring to go.' The big surprise is that sexual arousal is actually very fragile."

We commonly think of the brain as the center of reason, but raw sexual desire has its own logic, impulses and inner workings that follow a very different path than rational thought. In taking the care to recognize and engage with our desires, we see what in our natures might otherwise remain hidden — even from ourselves.

"We all have certain hidden instincts in ourselves, you know, stuff that we don't like really exposing to other people openly. And during sex, I think, would be the time to expose it all, just show it all. Kind of like showing your true self in a sexual way. So I would want to see that very fragile sense revealed." — Tarik

"Being of mixed race, I've always been different. But I've always attributed my difference to the outside things and not so much to what was going on inside.... Looking into oneself and being truthful and raw with oneself is scary." — Natasha

Swept Away Thomas Moore, who has written numerous books about the soul, encourages us to consider the metaphoric truths in mythology and art when trying to understand the irrational — and often conflicting — forces of desire within us. He told us, "You know, people are not really educated in the human passions. I've been interested in mythology for a long time because mythology gives us images and stories of how human beings behave and how they feel. And I think we need images and stories in order to know what's going on inside us."

As Moore conjures so memorably in his book *The Soul of Sex*, one of the most enduring and valuable figures we have for expressing the mysteries of arousal is the ancient Greek goddess of sex, Aphrodite. The Greeks regarded Aphrodite — ruler of the sexual realm — with so much importance, complexity and nuance that they used over four hundred names and a highly codified visual vocabulary to describe her.

Moore reminds us that the legend of Aphrodite's birth provides one of the most enduring and influential images of sexual arousal in history. Slick with sensuality, she rises up from the ocean — bold and bare and brazen, her skin dripping with promise. Aphrodite is the first lady of lust and libido, the original sex star. Floating toward us atop a gentle but forever-cresting wave, she literally embodies the emotion of being "swept away."

Aphrodite's classic pose has been imitated by Hollywood divas and backyard beauty queens of every generation. The sight of a woman emerging from the ocean has become virtually synonymous with sexual power.

"You might say it's the spirit of Aphrodite we experience when we feel sexual desire and sexual attraction," Moore told us. "It's as though suddenly Aphrodite appears and that spirit is present, you feel it, you're aware of it." And when she rises within us, our impulse is to reach out into the world and satisfy our hungers. Moore explains the image further:

"There's something about rising out
of the water that has a lot to do with our sexuality.
I think that's how we experience [it].
Our sexuality is vast, it's like a sea.
We don't know what it's about. It's as though we are
in a sea and there is all this beauty
and all this power…but still we have to be
individual and find our own way to be sexual
so as not to be in this vast ocean all the time."

When it comes to sexual ethics, however, Aphrodite doesn't have any. She's famously fickle and shamelessly selfish. Forget about lasting love or consequences or commitment. She's not waiting for Mr. Right. She wants Mr. Right Now! Moore tells us, "Aphrodite is specifically the goddess of sexual love. She's responsible for people coming together and making love. It's not in her interest that you remain married or loyal to someone forever. Her job is to make people desire each other."

Most of us know all too well the chaos that unbridled passion can bring into our lives. Jealousy and obsession, for example, are both manifestations of passion's dark side. A fifth-century philosopher put it well: "Desire doubled is love. Love doubled is madness." For all the bounty of pleasure that Aphrodite represents, her enormous potential to "cloud men's minds" was also to be feared. Feared — but not ignored.

In Erotic Art, *Eric Bentley provides illuminating comment on Agnolo Bronzino's* An Allegory on Venus and Cupid *(c. 1540–50): Venus and her son Cupid are locked in an illicit, incestuous embrace while Pleasure — the little boy to the right — is about to shower them with rose petals. Behind them, with the head of a little girl, is the serpent Deceit. She offers a honeycomb in one hand and conceals the sting in her tail with the other. Jealousy appears on the left, her face contorted with envy as she tears her hair. The whole scene would have been concealed, had not the forces of Truth and Time — the figures along the top of the painting — lifted the veiling blue drapery.*

Aphrodite's Wrath

According to myth, failing to pay proper homage to Aphrodite by celebrating her attributes in the world — such as sensuality and the existence of beauty — could be a costly oversight. When slighted, the goddess exacted revenge by inflicting offenders with twisted and debilitating erotic spells such as insatiable incestuous lust or, in the case of one poor character, outrageous passion for a bear! The lesson here is that if we utterly reject desire, we might be laying ourselves open to far more destructive passions.

Froma Zeitlin, who explores the dangerous side of Aphrodite in her groundbreaking work *Playing the Other*, explains that "according to the law regulating the logic of Greek Myth, any extreme attitude or form of behavior is countered exactly by its equally unacceptable reverse — and the offender is punished exactly according to the nature of the offense." Those who scorn Aphrodite are smitten in turn with transgressive, illicit or indelicate passions, impossible to fulfill. They may fall for a disastrous choice of love object. Or, as in the case of Narcissus, "when desire comes, it will turn not outward but rather within — to the self as an unattainable object of love."

As for the mysteries surrounding the onset of desire, Theresa Crenshaw, author of *The Alchemy of Love and Lust*, insightfully observes: "Fear and apprehension…inhibit desire as well as performance. Comfort enhances it. Newness inspires it. Tenderness promotes it. Danger and a sense of the forbidden intensify it. Then love enters the picture and confuses everything."

Invisible Threads Why do we go for the same types over and over? We only touch a hot stove once but can get burned again and again, searching for our heart's desire. The mysterious process that turns each of us on is universally recognizable, yet as individual as fingerprints.

Many experts believe that much of what we are drawn to — and run from — is based on embracing or rejecting what's in our past. Renowned psychiatric scholar Dr. Robert Stoller tells us that sexual arousal is not automatic but, rather, "a piece of theater whose story seems genuine and spontaneous because of the truth of the body's sensations." He sees the particular moment of erotic excitement "as a tangled, compacted mass — a microdot of scripts made up from impulses, desires, defenses, falsifications, truths avoided and memories of past events, erotic and nonerotic, going back to infancy." In other words, as Michael Bader explains, "If you take sexual arousal and you unpack it, you examine it from inside out and underneath, you find there's a lot of information there that happens in a moment."

Research tells us that we are each imprinted with what John Money first referred to as "a love map."

From the moment we are born, sounds, smells, tastes, when we felt threatened or safe, how our mothers sang to us, how our fathers laughed forge networks in our brain that channel and track our desires.

Over time, we create personal pathways to satisfaction that are filled with complexity and nuance.

Joann Ellison Rodgers writes in *Sex: A Natural History*: "In childhood, sexual teasing, roughhousing, contact sports, masturbating, kissing, cuddling with parents and imitating the sexual behavior of adults...is a rehearsal for the body and mind, necessary lessons for our brains as they prepare our bodies for sex." Eventually, our brains become wired with a maze of triggers and responses. When someone in view trips our wiring, the effects are immediate and profound.

That mysterious, surprising connection we sometimes feel with a person we've just met — "Are you sure we've never met before?" — may be because in our mind's eye we *have* met before. The idealized image of the perfect partner traced along invisible threads may closely match the person whose eyes, smile and mannerisms seem so familiar to us.

"To a large extent, we are projecting the person we hope to meet onto the person we are actually meeting," says psychologist Robert J. Sternberg. "Part of the excitement of the beginning of a relationship is exactly this projection — onto that real person standing in front of us — of what we hope the person will turn out to be."

"Girlfriends I know who are successful with dating services... [it's] usually because they have a type that they go for." — Kiisti

"I collected a lot of comic books when I was a kid so I was attracted to the muscle men in the mags. I guess that ties in to the type of guys I like. I'm not into the metrosexual, hair-product type guy. I like big guys. The guy with the wax in his hair and the flared jeans is not going to do it for me. I could probably break him in two!" — Natasha

"There are a few deal breakers or key elements that I've got to have in a guy. Height is one of them. Almost the taller, the better. But I also like broad shoulders. So sometimes you go too tall and you're not getting broad shoulders. Hands are really important.... Full lips are also an attractive feature. And I like dark-haired guys. Dark hair, curly hair, that does it for me. But that one's not a deal breaker. Because if it were a deal breaker, I think the dating would be kind of slim!" — Lisa

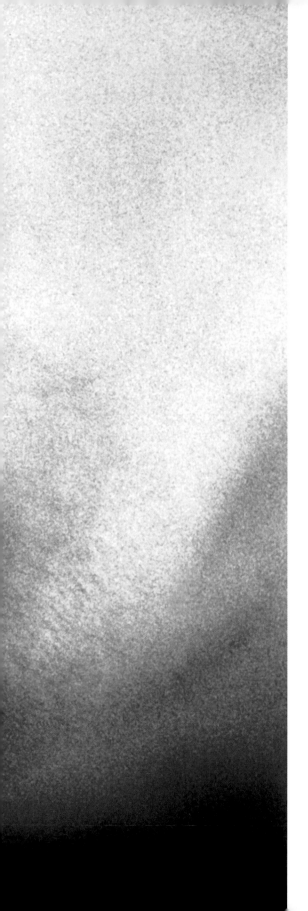

It's in His Kiss

Our appetite for kissing — sex's great hors d'oeuvre — seems to have its roots in early childhood and mother love. It is believed that mothers long ago fed their infants by transferring food mouth-to-mouth, like birds.

"To me, kissing somebody is more intimate than having sex. If I don't love a woman, I wouldn't kiss her. I mean, maybe at first or whatever, but... You know, a chick you've taken home.... To kiss her is... you're leading her on." — Antony

And there's more to this mouth-to-mouth intimacy than simply nourishment. As Thomas Moore tells us, "Some early writings say that when people kiss, they exchange the soul, that it's between their mouths and tongues that the soul is exchanged. And so the kiss is more of a soulful connection maybe than intercourse and other ways of being together. [A kiss] asks a lot from you. I think it asks a lot from a person to really kiss."

Love in the Time of Brain Scans

A fascinating study done in 2000 at University College, London, offers an unexpected answer to the age-old question: "What happens when we fall in love?" Researchers Andreas Bartles and Semir Seki took students who said they were madly in love and put them into a brain scanner to see what could be learned. What they found out was quite astonishing.

They discovered, first of all, that love activates an entirely different area of the brain than do other strong emotional states, such as anger and fear. It also employs neural mechanisms similar to those that generate the euphoria induced by drugs such as cocaine. Or, to put it another way — as *The Economist* did when it mentioned Bartles and Seki's research results in a recent article about the science of love — "The brains of people deeply in love do not look like those of people experiencing strong emotions but, instead, like those of people snorting coke!" In fact, the whole process of falling in love travels pathways very much associated with addiction (giving the bubble-gum song lyrics, "Hooked on a Feeling," a certain unexpected gravitas).

Helen Fisher, anthropologist and author of *Why We Love: The Nature and Chemistry of Romantic Love*, also studied brain scans and supports the notion that the brain part corresponding to love is more closely linked to primal drives, like hunger and thirst, than with emotions. Previous research had already found that the different stages of love — lust, romantic love and long-term attachment — are discernibly distinguishable neurological and biochemical phenomena. Lust, and its sexual cravings, are associated with testosterone; love, with dopamine, norepinephrine and serotonin; and attachment, with oxytocin and vasopressin.

In Fisher's evolutionary view of sex, these drives have been wired into our brains by millions of years of evolution. Lust propelled our ancestors to look for sex; romantic love forced them to focus their attention on one individual so that they weren't running around wasting time and energy; and attachment promoted living with one partner long enough to "rear a single child through infancy together."

Can lust trigger love? Helen Fisher thinks it can work both ways: "The chemistry of romantic love can trigger the chemistry of sexual desire. And the fuel of sexual desire can trigger the fuel of romance.... Although you intend to have casual sex, you might just fall in love." She theorizes that this may occur because the increasing levels of hormones connected with sex trigger the release of chemicals associated with romance.

"If you are fortunate," Fisher writes in *Why We Love*, "this magic

transforms itself into new feelings of security, comfort, calm and union with your partner." She believes that oxytocin and vasopressin — the "cuddle chemicals" that are released during orgasm — are involved in the stabilizing stage of love, what is called companionate love or attachment.

Sometimes, regardless of chemistry, attachment is difficult to achieve or sustain. The authors of *A General Theory of Love* believe that our culture encourages us to achieve rather than to attach. In their view, the long hours a couple spends working and acquiring often means too little time is left to spend with each other. "Advances in communication technology foster a false fantasy of togetherness," they write, "by transmitting the impression of contact…without its substance…. A culture wise in love's ways would understand a relationship's demand for time."

David Steinberg, who writes frequently on the culture and politics of sex and edited *The Erotic Impulse: Honoring the Sensual Self*, tells us, "Much as we would like to believe that we can jump in and out of erotic and sexual encounters as easily as we can jump in and out of a shower, a movie or a subway, the experience of being sexual in full, rich, powerful ways inevitably engages an entire range of complex issues — emotionally and spiritually." Some of these issues include our feelings about interpersonal boundaries, past experiences and giving up control. And yet it is precisely because sex has the potential to challenge us on all these levels that its gifts can be so great.

As in so many things, knowing yourself well has its rewards. In a 2003 Cornell University study, evolutionary biologists Peter Buston and Stephen Emlen suggested that people think of themselves as certain types and choose partners to match. Those who are able to assess themselves accurately and pick partners with complementary traits (ranging from appearance to personality, education and financial status) tend to have longer relationships. The type of early bond we form with our parents, many psychologists say, can also influence the type of attachments we make as adults.

Men and women's attachment styles range from "secure" (those who see themselves and others in a positive way and enjoy intimacy) to "insecure" (those who believe they are unworthy of love and consider other people untrustworthy and rejecting). Fortunately, for those whose relationship with their parents was less than stellar, it is believed the early parental bond makes up only one small part of an ever-changing love map.

Story Time

Why do we fall in and out of love, in and out of relationships? Psychologist Robert Sternberg has searched for the answers to these questions for many years. In his latest theory, he proposes that love is a story. "Each of us has an ideal story about love and it may be the most important thing we learn about ourselves," he says.

In something similar to the love maps theory, we usually fall in love with someone whose story is the same or similar to ours. The focus here, though, is not on our personal history but on our personal view of love.

"A couple's stories of what love is and what it should be may or may not coincide," Sternberg writes in *Love Is a Story*. "For example, if someone wants to live a romantic fairy tale but finds herself actually living in a war story, she is likely to be dissatisfied. Others prefer the war story and would feel bored out of their minds in the romantic fairy tale."

Looking at past relationships, Sternberg suggests, is a way to help us understand our ideal story. What attributes do the people to whom we felt most attracted have in common with us? What about the ones to whom we felt least attracted? "It is important to remember," he adds, "that in close relationships, love is part, but not all, of what leads to success. A supportive environment, friendships, economic well-being, spiritual fulfillment and compatible interests and values all make a difference, too."

The writer Antoine de Saint-Exupéry expresses
this simply and beautifully:
"Love does not consist in gazing at each other
but in looking outward together in the same direction."

What's Love Got to do with It?

Love, in all its complexity and irrationality, has not always held the value it does today as a directional guide in life. In the fascinating history *Love in the Ancient World*, authors Christopher Miles and John Julius Norwich tell us, "For the ancients, love did not make you better. It made you worse." In fact, the Roman comedies depict men in love as witless slaves of their mistresses — men who have forfeited the independence that Romans held most dear.

In the city that gave romance its name, it would have been considered the height of frivolity to marry the person you love. Roman marriages were unashamedly about amassing fortune, having children and creating strategic alliances. This was not to say that married couples never loved each other — they often did — but even marital love took a back seat to the pursuit of power and finance. "People got divorced when the political winds changed — which was often," Miles and Norwich point out.

And just as political winds change, so do our attitudes about sex. I suppose there will always be some people for whom sex continues to be all about making babies. Others completely disassociate the two. And then there are those who pursue making babies without having sex at all! Today, sex is seen as a potent agent of commerce and is used to sell, sell, sell.

Thirty thousand years ago, people viewed an image of the vulva as a gateway to God. Today, it's more likely to be referred to as "the money shot."

It's a loss to us when sex becomes dehumanized. At the heart of mutual gratification lie empathy and compassion. Still, many people today find it helpful to approach sex with some level of functional pragmatism. Long-standing relationships and sexual ardor are not always the most natural bedfellows.

"Well, ideally, it would be perfect to have love and sex together and find it through one person and live that way. However, it doesn't really happen so in messy reality. I'm able to have sex with someone without having any kind of emotional connection. Without feeling love. And that is totally acceptable." — Tarik

"I don't know what the name of that Indian goddess is, but she has eight arms. And I'd be with someone and I'd have two of them around them — but my other six would be, you know, reaching out to other people and always looking for somebody else, for something else." — Cayra

It sometimes happens that emotional claustrophobia can get in the way of sexual arousal. Michael Bader gave us a remarkable insight when he told us,

"There's this tension in all of us when we have sex — between something that's a very intimate, intense connection to the other and a requirement that we be able to focus inward and privilege our own pleasure. If you're worried too much or focused too much on your partner, you sometimes can't surrender to your own pleasure, you can't turn selfish enough to be able to really let go. Sex is about letting go."

Chapter Four
Fantasy

Each of us has unique triggers for arousal.
And when those are set off, it's heaven.
Absolute heaven! The rest of the time,
we've gotta do it for ourselves — in fantasies,
from the most basic to the elaborate. Imagination is
the single most potent engine driving sexual desire.

"A lot of guys probably want two women. That's always a huge sexual fantasy. Would I be into that? Sure, why not? What the heck, try it once. See what happens. I think I'll take one for all the guys and say that that's probably the number one fantasy...." — Roland

"The idea of being watched. I don't know why that's such a turn-on. That's kind of odd, I don't know, I can't explain why that would turn me on." — Cayra

"Well I guess for every gay guy, the usual fantasy would be this big, huge orgy. That would definitely be a fantasy. In actual life, could I ever do that? No, I could never do that!" — Tarik

Research has found that in fantasy scenarios, women are more likely to create complex narratives containing detailed personal characteristics, while men tend to focus more on physical attributes. For women, the action frequently unfolds slowly, while in men's fantasies, it often happens fast. But the opposite can be true too. In fact, when it comes to sexual fantasies, there are no rules. Perhaps that's why we sometimes find our fantasies confusing.

How many powerful people have
been baffled by a domination fantasy?
Or what about imagining we are
the opposite sex?

And some fantasies are, well,
just plain odd
— even to the person creating them....

Consider masturbation — which everyone has. Why do some of us still feel a twinge of guilt? Ask people what they think about during solo sex and you may uncover where the guilty feelings come from. It's not what's happening *below* the waist but *above* the shoulders that causes worry. Some of this confusion might disappear if we understand that having a fantasy is not a form of planning ahead!

People who study sexual fantasies all stress that the arousing secret life that pops up unbidden in the privacy of our minds is a natural, healthy part of our sexuality — a sign that our imaginations are alive and well.

Wendy Maltz, the co-author of *Private Thoughts*, views effective sexual fantasies as "nature's built-in aphrodisiac. They can be used to boost sexual response, "sort of like a vibrator of the mind."

Michael Bader believes that having fantasies is something we are evolutionarily primed to be able to do in order to achieve sexual arousal successfully, despite acquired social inhibitions. "That's how sexual fantasies work," he told us. "Arousal depends on our creating situations in our minds that help reverse or overcome the kind of stories that normally keep us repressed or down."

Leda and the Swan
The seduction of Leda by the god Zeus, disguised as a swan, has been depicted in many works of art, including this marble sculpture by Bartolomeo Ammannati. The Greek myth combines many of the elements of fantasies — including powerful seducer, helpless maiden, and forces of nature and magic beyond social control. Its eroticism is fueled by the notion that Zeus's desire for Leda is so powerful that it literally transforms him.

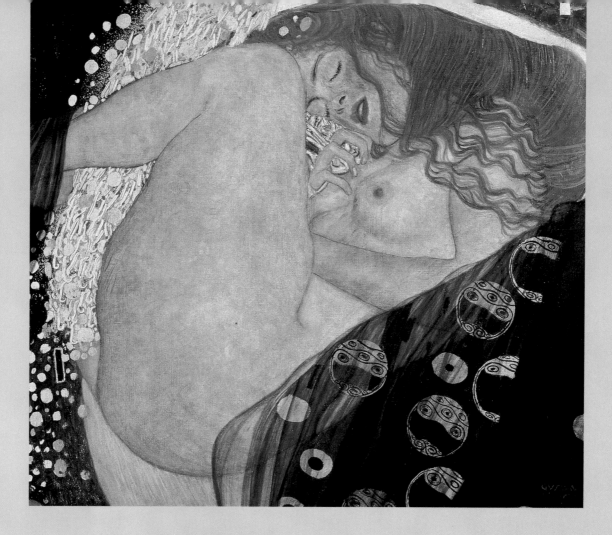

Bashing the Bishop, Polishing the Pearl

For as long as people have masturbated, those in charge have been trying to make them stop. Maggie Paley makes this point saliently and with characteristic wit in The Book of the Penis. *She recounts that when the Roman Catholic Church in eighth-century Europe published a series of penitential books describing sexual misdeeds and their penalties, masturbation was allotted more space than any other sin. By way of example, the Church pointed to Onan — a figure from Genesis who was put to death for spilling his seed on the ground. (The use of the word "onanism" as a synonym for masturbation survives to this day.)*

Ironically, Paley tells us, poor Onan was not masturbating. He was actually practising coitus interruptus — *what is commonly referred to as "pulling out." It's likely that Onan "pulled out" to avoid breaking the law of begetting a child with the widow of his brother. There is actually no prohibition against masturbation — or any mention of it — in the Bible.*

Like love maps, sexual fantasies reflect our personal history and culture. According to Bader, "Men often grow up thinking sexual pleasure is OK if you're in the dominant role but it's embarrassing or shameful if you like having a finger up your anus." Yet, despite feeling inhibited or uncomfortable with certain kinds of sexuality, most of us still want to experience them. "Our sexual fantasies give us the best of both worlds," Bader says. "We get to feel sexually aroused but at the same time we don't have to feel guilty or worry about rejection."

Wendy Maltz compares sexual fantasies to "risk-free playgrounds" — a safe place to go in our minds.

"When my self-esteem is low, I have these fantasies of women approaching me, wanting to have sex with me. It's an ego boost for me to have these kinds of fantasies. I never act on them. All I need is to imagine some stranger thinking I'm hot and that makes me feel better." — Cayra

Awareness of the sensory elements conjured by our imaginations in fantasy can provide clues to our individual erotic natures. And what we learn about ourselves can be used to enhance our sexual pleasure — alone, or with a partner. But what about the disturbing or frightening fantasies, the ones that seem to run counter to how we think of ourselves?

As we reflect on our fantasies, it's important to understand that they are not motivated by rational impulses. They enrich us most not because they're a call for action but, rather, because they open us to the deeper mysteries of sex and our individuality.

Thomas Moore gave us an enormously freeing insight when he told us, "Fantasies, when they come naturally to us, are poetry. They mean something more than what they seem to mean. We're supposed to look more deeply into them. Images of violence or rape or kinky kinds of things that you wouldn't want to talk about with people you know? Even those dark fantasies have something to offer."

He suggests that when those kinds of images come along, we "don't take them quite so literally but take them as a little poetry, expressing something positive."

"Sex has to be consensual, the whole thing has to be consensual, and that's why it scares me that maybe there's a part of me that's sort of primordial that way. You know, cave woman, knocked on the head and taken from behind.... I would never consciously condone that, or even seek that out. And that's what's scary. Because I'm not sure what that means." — Natasha

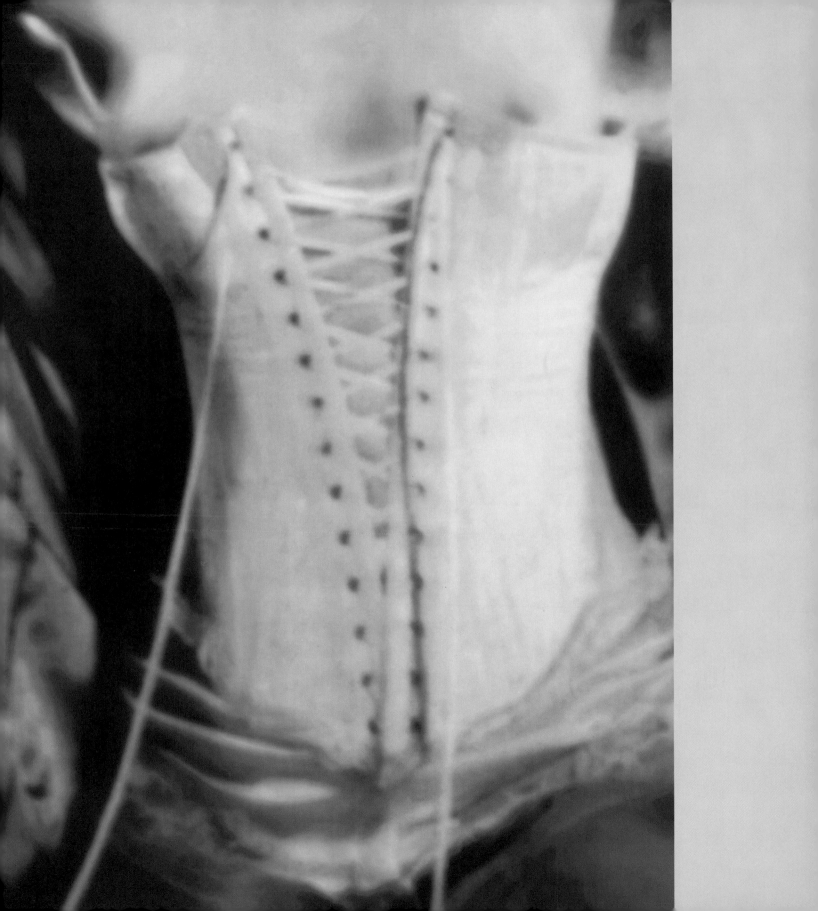

From Fantasy to Fetish

A stiletto heel, a studded collar, a balloon, a plush doll... When an inanimate object not only arouses our desire but also becomes an erotic necessity, we have entered fetish territory. Fetishes typically focus on clothing — either the material used to make it (leather, rubber, fur, silk) or the form it takes (high-heeled shoes, panties, corsets). A fetish object can also be a body part — an attribute made so important that the rest of the individual disappears. A fetishist's triggers are imbued with symbolism. Think of the woman attracted to "bad boys" who wear leather and ride motorcycles: it's what the man in all his gear represents that cranks her libido.

The Secret Life of Shoes

The hidden meaning attached to a certain fetish object can sometimes be as surprising as the fetish itself. Take the high-heeled shoe, for example — a fetish classic. Women might love the way a high shoe extends their leg and sets off a beautiful outfit, but the signals our stilettos are sending can be a bit more complex.

Michael Bader gave us some interesting insights into the secret life of shoes: "A spiked heel is a phallic image and, for a man, it often symbolizes a woman who is powerful, strong and dominant (even if it doesn't feel that way to the woman). In other words, a woman in high heels is one he doesn't have to worry about; he can do whatever he wants with her, and doesn't have to feel responsible for her."

In Sexy Origins and Intimate Things, *Charles Panati traces the history of the stiletto heel. "The word* stiletto, *dating from around 1611, is Italian for 'small dagger' — a short, slender knife. In America, the first recorded use of the term 'stiletto heel' occurred in 1953 to describe "a high, thin heel narrower than a spike heel." Panati humorously notes — browsing a video store on a tree-lined, Long Island street — that titles such as* Foot Worship, Stiletto Sluts, High-heeled Dominatrix, Dykes in Spikes, Eastern Foot Torture *and* Toe Fucks *were easy to come by. But there was absolutely nothing on the eroticism of men's shoes and feet. "No tapes entitled* Studs in Construction Boots, Pretty Boys in Penny Loafers, Blond Surfers in Smelly Sneakers. Apparently," *Panati concludes, "women just aren't sexually into men's shoes or feet."*

Tie Me Up, Tie Me Down

Research has shown that by far the most common fantasy involves some form of dominance and submission. Not necessarily the kind with whips and chains and the requisite theatrical clichés, but some scenario in which one person has more control than the other one. Odd — given that most of us strive for equality and balance in modern relationships.

Michael Bader sheds some much-needed light on this darker side of ourselves by suggesting that there's a deeper motivation for fantasy scenarios that run counter to the social goals we strive for in life. He told us about a woman who "described sexual excitement like a wave crashing on the shore, and she said you have to be sure that the shore can take it. That it's sturdy, that you don't have to be worried, 'Is he happy? Did he come? Does he think I'm great?' If any of those thoughts are there, even subtly, it dampens sexual arousal. So, our unconscious minds are amazing instruments. And we find a way to overcome those inhibitions through developing sexual fantasies."

> *"Yes, women have fantasies. Do we share them? Do we talk about it? I don't know.*
> *If I talked about mine, if I told people what my fantasies were like, they'd want to arrest me! And that's the way I like it!"* — Betty Dodson

Wendy Maltz believes there's a risk involved in enacting our fantasies. "I think they're fantasies for a reason. When you move them out of the realm of your own mind and try and impose them on a partner or encourage a partner to act them out, people can end up feeling very disappointed and humiliated. Sometimes it does result in pleasant surprises and is very positive. But that's only when the people involved can communicate well and know what they're doing. And when the emotional connection in the relationship always remains what's most important — not the acting out of a certain scenario."

For those who feel safe unlocking the door to the secret room upstairs, sharing fantasies can be a way to find out about the erotic nature of your partner and his or her inner life. Perhaps this will add a new dimension to lovemaking or to your relationship. "The unknown gets the adrenaline flowing," Betty Dodson told us. "And that can feed into sexual arousal, boosting desire for both partners. But," she cautions, "if one of you dislikes doing something, drop it. There are so many other things to explore."

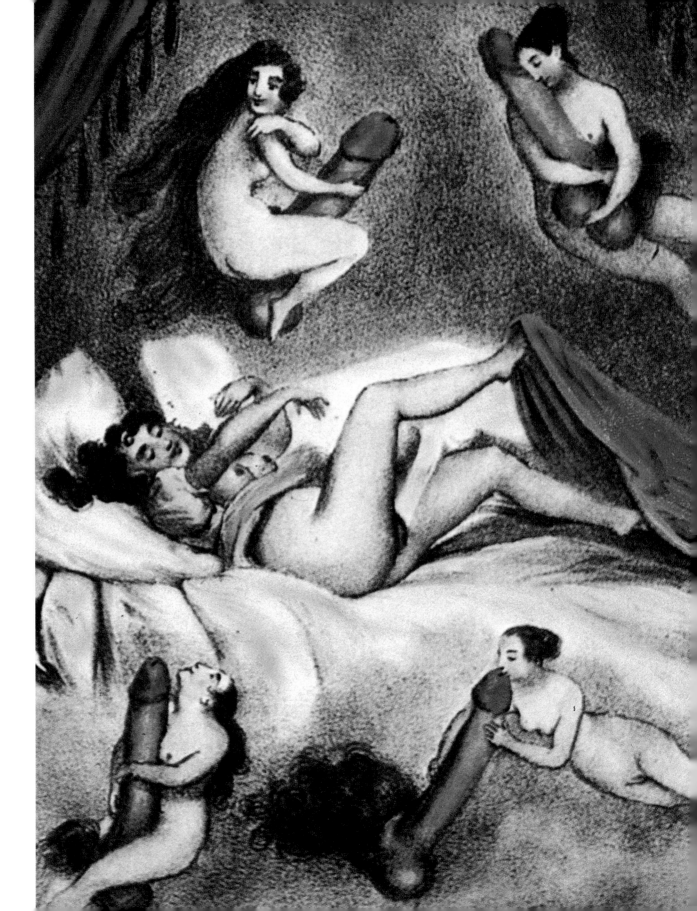

Lust and Laughter

If sexual fantasies are imagination's answer to inhibition, a sense of humor is its secret weapon. As Michael Bader explains, "We feel guilty and ashamed of sex. And so what jokes do is play on our guilt and our shame, make us laugh and enable us to enjoy [sex]. It's a form of mastery. You know, people who tell jokes, it's often a way they have of getting on top of a situation that in some way bothers or threatens them."

Humor and eroticism are linked, Bader tells us, because "both have a delightful ending. And because we don't know how we get there. Because the process of getting there is mysterious. As with sex, a joke has a build-up, there's foreplay and then there's a climax to it. And the climax is often surprising. If it's not surprising, it's not funny. And it results in a sudden release."

People who laugh spontaneously at the moment of climax combine two brief but freeing sensations. In both orgasm and laughter, we give ourselves up to the moment. The body's desire for joy is satisfied by our surrender to it.

Bringing a sense of childlike creativity and fun into our sexual lives takes sex in a different direction — or perhaps it just takes us back. As children we are naturally earthy, naturally bawdy. We enjoy "gross out" humor and "playing doctor." But if we grow up in a family that's not sex-positive, childhood silliness can have negative consequences. If we learn early in our lives to disconnect sex from play, we may miss out on the part of a sexual experience that can put a smile on our face.

"Much of lovemaking's preludes are 'neotonous,'" writes Joann Ellison Rodgers in *Sex: A Natural History*, "a throwback to the joy and playfulness we experienced as children — nakedness, body contact, laughing and rolling around...." Putting the givens of safe sex and reproductive precautions aside for a moment, is it possible to take sex too seriously? Wendy Maltz thinks so. "I see so many couples who approach sex seriously and that's one of their biggest problems. They don't know how to laugh about it. And sex *is* awkward and messy at times and doesn't always work out well. In therapy sessions, I often get people to see how amusing sex is and how funny we are. We need to approach life with a sense of humor because in many ways it's so absurd."

Lust and laughter trump fear and shame. In fact, we see the powerful link between sex and comedy played out in countless forms of boundary-bursting burlesque.

In his stunning book, *Roman Sex,* John Clarke explains that the giant phalluses and the phallic gods of Rome — Priapus and Hermaphrodites in particular — derived much of their power from the giggles they engendered. "If the surprise of the double-take is the stuff of all humor, they are supremely funny."

Boundary-bursting Burlesque Babes

Gypsy Rose Lee (1911–1970)

It's been said that Gypsy Rose Lee didn't bother waiting for the world to define her; instead, she created her own niche and changed the world. The philosopher H.L. Mencken coined the term "ecdysiast," meaning "striptease artist," to describe her as she transformed the act of stripping into a display of intellect and wit. Notoriously self-reliant, Gypsy's been quoted as saying, "Praying is like a rocking chair: it'll give you something to do but won't get you anywhere." She wrote novels and a play, starred in films and became a television celebrity. Her autobiography Gypsy *inspired Stephen Sondheim to write a Broadway play about her life.*

Lili St. Cyr (1918–1999)

During the forties and fifties, Lili St. Cyr elevated voyeurism to a high art — dazzling audiences as she invited them to watch her take a bath or do a reverse striptease, by dressing, on stage. Trained as a ballerina, she incorporated classical mythology, fantasy and a sense of cultural sophistication in her act. As one admiring critic noted, "While others were taking it off, Lili was often putting it on — and the results were no less tantalizing." In the much-loved swimming pool scene from The Rocky Horror Picture Show, *Janet Weiss, in her ode to decadence, sings: "God bless Lili St. Cyr!"*

Josephine Baker (1906–1975)

Josephine Baker first set herself apart on stage clowning, mugging and improvising at the end of a long chorus line. In time, her "fooling around" evolved into a revolutionary stage presence combining nudity, jazz and comedy in ways no one had ever seen. Descended from Apalachee Indians and Black slaves, Baker's childhood reflected the hardships associated with bigotry in America. In Paris, she became the darling of Europe's cultural elite. She was decorated for her undercover work with the French Resistance during World War II and became a civil rights activist in the 1960s, helping integrate Las Vegas nightclubs.

Mae West (1893–1980)

"To err is human — but it feels divine!" Groundbreaking blonde bombshell, sex clown and queen of the innuendo-laced one-liners, Mae West married sex and comedy with unstoppable style that helped launch every successive form of popular entertainment — from Vaudeville, to Burlesque, to Broadway and Hollywood. In 1926, Mae wrote, produced and directed the Broadway show Sex, *and was promptly arrested for obscenity. The following year, her new play,* Drag, *was banned on Broadway because its subject matter was homosexuality. Her classic line, "When I'm bad, I'm better," aptly described her trailblazing career.*

The "cheekiness of the backside" brings us back to the side of guess who? Our siren of sex, the diva of desire — Aphrodite. The lifting of the skirt was traditionally part of her bawdy dance.

In his inspirational decoding of Aphrodite's gestures, Thomas Moore illuminates, "It's a little bit like a can-can. It's lifting up the dress for fun — a peek-a-boo approach to the body — and people understood that in the worship of Aphrodite, the goddess of sex, this has its place. It's something essential. It's not a deviancy to be vulgar about sex. It's a celebration of life."

We reach past inhibitions, we experiment, we overstep, we break the rules and create new ones, displaying what is private and exposing what we normally protect. Simultaneously, we connect to our deepest nature and are transported beyond ourselves.

The impulse of voyeurism finds expression in film, fashion, dance

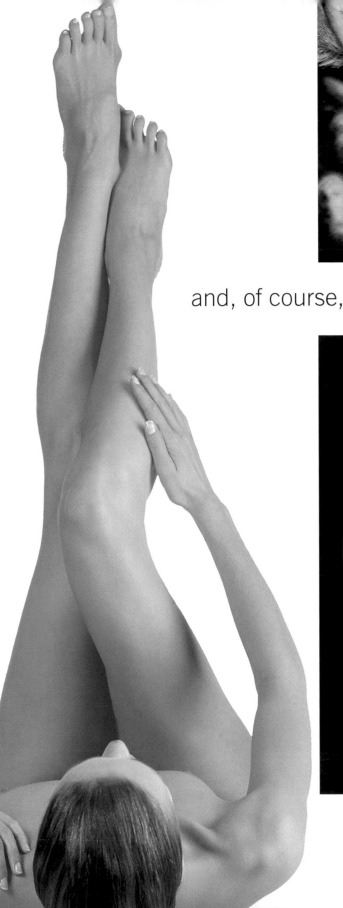

and, of course, the artful striptease.

"E" is for Erotic

Sexual arousal, whether it involves romance or pure lust, is highest when there is a tension between the attraction pulling us toward the partner and one or more barriers standing in the way," psychologist Jack Morin writes in *The Erotic Mind*. His four "cornerstones of eroticism" are longing and anticipation, violating prohibitions, searching for power and overcoming ambivalence.

Distance really *does* seem to make the heart grow fonder. Phone conversations, text messages and emails can burn up the lines between us when we're apart, making our eventual reunions all the more combustible. "Anything that encourages partners to take each other for granted is the enemy of longing," writes Morin. "You can kiss anticipation goodbye if you get into one of those over-close, clingy relationships where the partners give up their rights to be separate individuals…. Time apart, vigorous disagreements and occasional fair fights all re-establish individuality and can fan the flames of desire."

Desire likes extremes — fast and slow, naughty and nice, dominant

Overcoming sexual taboos intensifies arousal, as does playing power games when safety is assured. "The power scenario most frequently mentioned by both men and women is surrendering to a super-aroused, aggressive partner," says Morin. "Peak encounters often occur at the critical juncture when ambivalent reluctance gives way to passion." Trying a new sexual technique or being simultaneously attracted and repelled by someone are two examples.

"Sometimes just a hint of naughtiness, a tease of anticipation, a whisper of domination is just the right amount," Morin says.

And keeping ourselves a little off-balance also helps. "There doesn't even have to be foreplay," a lesbian interview told us. "One of the ways I enjoy having sex with my girlfriend is with our clothes on, just using our hands, standing up usually. And it's quite quick, not violent but intense."

and passive. It thrives on variety, wilts on same-old, same-old.

Chapter Five
Release

In sex, as in anything creative, we're most fulfilled
when open to experimentation and
to broadening our aesthetics and our sense of
place in the world. In heightened arousal,
we teeter on a precipice outside ordinary experience.

*"I think you have to take a risk in order to find out about yourself,
find out about that person. You're not going to find out anything
if you don't risk anything. You're not going to go anywhere if
you don't risk anything. You're not going to leave your house if
you don't risk anything."* — Kiisti

*"The journey during sex is what's important rather than just
something that is very strict, regimented, you know, it starts here,
we reach climax and then it's done and one person falls asleep
(we all know who that is!) and the other person stays awake and
thinks about the meaning of life."* — Lisa

The French have an expression for orgasm
— *le petit mort*, the little death. In dying, we let go of this
world and all its limitations. Losing ourselves clears
a space for something larger. In sexual release,
we sense a communion with the realm of the divine.
As we touch each other, we truly touch something timeless.

Sex is like a form of ritual. Thomas Moore suggests that sex, in the ways it causes us to disengage from the ordinary, can act almost as "the mysterious rite" at the center of a relationship.

"Sex is completely different now that I'm in love," one of our interviews told us. "When I wasn't in love, it was just pure physical sensation. When love is involved, there's a balance of body, mind and spirit that enables me to be confident and to enjoy my life to the fullest."

"In the middle of an orgasm, try to stop. You can't!" — Antony

"The shock. Ah! My feet are curling, you know!" — Tarik

"It wipes my mind clean." — Natasha

"All boundaries are destroyed." — Tarik

"Something that transports you." — Kiisti

"It's transcendent, really." — Natasha

"You're about to collide into something and there's this, like, bam!" — Tarik

"Darkness. And pure, just sort of, blank." — Natasha

If sex is the religion of a relationship, we celebrate with our own rituals that connect us with the sensual, elemental side of life: candles, the fire; baths, the water; perfume, the air; food, the earth and the gifts it brings.

German poet Rainer Maria Rilke once wrote about sex: "Physical pleasure is a sensual experience no different from pure seeing or the pure sensation with which a fine fruit fills the tongue...."

When we eat without paying attention to what we're eating or how it's been prepared, we rob ourselves of pleasure.

Sexual pleasure works the same way. Eroticism is a subtle magic. Just as an understanding of how ingredients work together leads to more creative cooking, so an awareness of desire's many nuances will make sex more satisfying. It may even summon a sense of the divine. Through love, the body becomes a doorway to the divine. In fact, our body is the gateway to everything in this world — for the body expresses the spirit.

"After sex, if we're taking a shower together, I would feel that it's my responsibility to clean, to wash that person's body. Not only mine but that person's body. Kind of taking care of it, as if it's my body." — Tarik

The Shape of My Heart
Metaphorically
speaking, hearts come
 in all shapes and sizes
— generous, full,
 broken, cold, prickly,
bleeding, bursting,
 lighter than air. Some
are hard to find and
 many are hard to figure
out. The lovely symbol
 for the heart is
universally recognized. Its swollen, chubby, rounded top is ripe

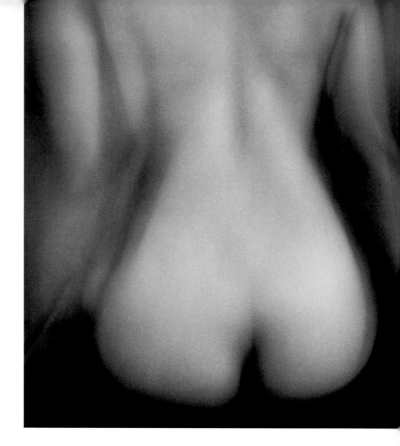

and swooning, while the point it teeters on pledges not to budge
from being near. The symbol is ancient and may
not be traceable to a
single source —
but the human
form certainly offers
some compelling
proof of
inspirational origin.

Love is all around You

In his book, *Eros: The Myth of Ancient Greek Sexuality*, Bruce Thorton cites the earliest origin of Eros as one of the primary forces of the Universe. Eros is not only known to be "implicated in all the desires and appetites in every living creature" but is also a primary force of nature and magnetism defining the cosmos. According to later legend, Eros came into being as the love child of Aphrodite (the great goddess of sex) and Mars (the aggressive god of war). Thorton talks about the ambiguity that is at the heart of Eros — one who creates pain as well as pleasure, violence as well as connection, volatile emotional chaos but also cultivated domestic order.

In an ancient Greek story, humans were originally paired in perfect globes, happily rolling about the countryside. But when they tried to go up to Olympus, Zeus cut them in half and, for the rest of time, people have searched for their missing half.

"Sexual energy, creative energy, it's all the same thing. You know, love, sex…it's just expression. And sometimes it ends up being a baby and sometimes it ends up being a comic book And sometimes it ends up being a painting or a song." — Kiisti

"I think you can be sexually connected to anybody. Male or female. I think sex can be that all-encompassing. But when you add your soul, your spirit or deepest feelings and emotions, that's when you really can enter this next step of being with somebody and exploring yourself as well." — Cayra

Classics scholar and poet Anne Carson writes that the Greek word *eros* means "desire for that which is missing." According to Carson, eros is about magnetism and boundaries, including "the boundary of flesh and self between you and me." It is only at the moment when we want to dissolve that boundary that we realize we never can. Love, to the ancient Greeks (and to many of us), is bittersweet. But no less sought-after because of it.

Thomas Moore told us: "There is a dimension of sex beyond what goes on in lovemaking and being a sexual partner.

The Greeks said that the world itself began in Eros… and Eros means "connection." So that for the Greeks, the fact that the moon stays close to the Earth is an erotic activity. There's almost a love relationship between our moon and the Earth.

That's a notion that…may be strange to modern minds," Moore mused, "but I think it's a beautiful idea that the whole world is connected by an erotic principle. And a great deal of creative life comes out of the connection between things."

Sam Keen writes in *To Love and Be Loved* that it is a mistake to think that two individuals have sex in a vacuum. He believes we should focus on acquiring the skills that will make us into loving people rather than focusing on choosing the right partner. "First cultivate a life filled with compassion, and passion will be added to it.... The best way to become a good sexual partner is to concentrate on becoming a loving human being. Practice paying attention, listening, empathy, compassion, sensuality."

When sex has hurt us, we may find it extremely difficult to find a way to re-engage with it, or to ascertain what value it can continue to have in our lives. The nature of arousal is so ephemeral, that even if we have not been

"If I'm with an individual and I see that they are holding back for some reason, I'm more interested in finding out what that reason is...trying to figure out why they're vulnerable and what their fears are.... The sex can wait. We don't have to partake, we don't have to have it." — Roland

> *"Sex is an important part in looking for love just because sex is such an important element in a loving relationship for me. Now I know that there are definitely marriages that from the outside appear to work, and they talk about the modern-day sexless marriage. Relationships ebb and flow and the sex in a relationship ebbs and flows. But, hopefully, it's not a tap that ever goes to the fully 'off' position. At least not in my life."* — Lisa

hurt or received any trauma, we may slip into complacency, where our expectations for sex become so lowered that we stop assigning any real value to it in our daily lives — and the whole raw theater of it seems more and more ridiculous. There are times when disengaging from sexual activity for a time is the best thing we can do for ourselves.

The most important kind of nourishment we get from sex is not necessarily found in the act of having it — but rather in appreciating its sources.

If sex becomes shameful, dysfunctional or wrought with fear, our desires can provide a window on what needs healing. Sex focuses us on other people and allows love to be expressed.

Thomas Moore talked to us at length about the mysteries and complexities of sex. He reminded us that the intimacy we get from music, art, literature, film and a life motivated by love all play an important part in reinvigorating our imaginations and sustaining us on our sexual journey. Sexual desire can be summoned — and even satisfied — by nature's beauty, the love of friends, good food or by some form of creative engagement with the world.

As Mary Anne Mohanraj writes in the introduction to *Aqua Erotica*, "People are different during sex. In sex, we are most naked — mentally and emotionally as well as physically…. We hope, when we lay ourselves bare before another, that he or she will match us in this risky game and lay themselves open as well. That is the lure of intimacy, the promise of shared fears that may be overcome by desire."

— it nurtures, it burns.

Its heat is irresistible.
It takes us out of ourselves even
as it takes us deeper into ourselves.
By cultivating and
understanding our desires and
their satisfactions, we connect
to our deepest nature, to the
sensuality of life and
to each other.

Editorial Notes and Credits

7: Naomi Kaltman / CORBIS OUTLINE

11: Photograph by Colin Bell.

Chapter One

12: Herbert Draper, *The Gates of Dawn*, 1900. By permission of akg-images, London. Herbert Draper (1863–1920) is among the best-known of the Victorian Classicist painters. His works, inspired by the art and mythology of Classical Greece and Rome, are highly dramatic and sensually charged narratives featuring beautiful maidens and dynamic heroes.

14: Excerpted from the documentary *Kim Cattrall: Sexual Intelligence*.

15: Viagra pill. Wyman Ira / CORBIS SYGMA.

16: Original source unknown. This image, called "Life Explained," is a favorite on countless Web sites — and no wonder. What better way to sum up the fundamental difference between women and men?

17: Excerpted from the documentary *Kim Cattrall: Sexual Intelligence*.

18: April / Getty Images.

20: Spencer Jones / PictureArts / CORBIS.

21: Linda Holt Ayriss / Getty Images.

22: Excerpted from the documentary *Kim Cattrall: Sexual Intelligence*.

23: John Singer Sargent, *Figure Study*, c.1900. Watercolor and pencil on paper. By permission of the National Museums & Galleries of Wales. Although Sargent (1856–1925) is widely known as one of the great portraitists of the late nineteenth and early twentieth centuries, his paintings and drawings of male nudes were long hidden from the public eye. These are sensuous, languid, beautifully rendered works by a master whose influences included the Impressionists and the brilliant Spanish painter Diego Velázquez.

25: Michelangelo Buonarroti, *David*, 1501–04. Marble (detail). Galleria dell'Accademia, Florence, Italy. By permission of the Bridgeman Art Library. This superb sculpture, considered one of Michelangelo's (1475–1564) greatest works, portrays the Biblical David at the moment that he decides to engage Goliath. It is based on the artistic discipline of *disegno*, which is built on knowledge of the male human form. Under this discipline, sculpture is considered to be the finest form of art because it mimics divine creation. Because Michelangelo adhered to the concepts of *disegno*, he worked under the premise that the image of David was already in the block of marble he was shaping — in much the same way as the human soul is thought to be found within the physical body.

26: Kim Cattrall near Cerne Abbas, Dorset, England — with the Cerne Abbas Giant in the background. Courtesy of photographer Colin Bell.

27: Patrick Ward / CORBIS.

28: Photographs of phallic art in Pompeii by Michael Larvey, from *Roman Sex* by John R. Clarke and Michael Larvey. By permission of Michael Larvey and John R. Clarke.

29: Kim Cattrall in Pompeii, with tintinnabula. Courtesy of photographer Colin Bell.

30: *Priapus*, from the Casa dei Vettii (House of the Vettii), c.50–79 A.D. Roman fresco, Pompeii. By permission of the Bridgeman Art Library.

31: Figure of *Narcissus* (detail), parian porcelain modelled by E.B. Stephens, after John Gibson. Made by William Copeland for the Art Union of London, 1846. By permission of the Victoria & Albert Picture Library. The invention in the 1840s of parian porcelain — a perfect imitation of marble, both in color and in tint — heralded the mass production of sculpture and allowed the Victorian middle classes to possess articles of high art. The Minton pottery coined the word "Parian" to suggest Paros, the Greek isle that furnished much of the stone used in the Classical period. The Art Union's order for parian models of John Gibson's marble statue of *Narcissus* was the first major commission of parian statuary porcelain. Note the strategically placed fig leaf.

32: Edouard Manet, *Le Déjeuner sur l'Herbe*, 1863. Oil on canvas. Musée d'Orsay, Paris, France. By permission of the Bridgeman Art Library. Not surprisingly, this now-famous work by Edouard Manet (1832–1883) sparked a public outcry when it was unveiled in 1863. Art patrons howled at the alleged indecency of two fully dressed men appearing in the company of a naked female bather.

33: (top left and right, and lower right) Photograph of erotic murals by Antonia Mulas, from *Eros in Pompeii: The Erotic Art Collection of the Museum of Naples* by Michael Grant and Antonia Mulas. By permission of Antonia Mulas. (Lower left) *Mars and Venus*. Roman fresco from Pompeii. Museo Archeologico Nazionale, Naples, Italy. Photograph by Erich Lessing / Art Resource, NY.

35: Kim Cattrall in Pompeii. Courtesy of photographer Colin Bell.

36: Animation by Laura Shepherd, Sam Javanrouh, Mike Brown and Justin Mencel. Courtesy of Optix Digital Pictures, Toronto. Excerpted from the documentary *Kim Cattrall: Sexual Intelligence*.

37: Gustave Courbet, *The Origin of the World*, 1866. Oil on canvas. Photo: Hervé Lewandowski. Musée d'Orsay, Paris, France. By permission of Réunion des Musées Nationaux / Art Resource, NY. Gustave Courbet (1819–1877), who believed emphatically in painting only real and existing things, became a rallying cry for a new generation of French artists during the 1850s. His bold and original works shocked the public with their subject matter as well as their size. The *Origin of the World* is a brilliant example of his artistic risk-taking.

38: (top) This carving of a vulva was found in a cave in Sergeac, France, and is believed to date from about 30,000 B.C. Musée des Antiquités Nationales, France. (Bottom) Hand-colored fashion plate by Alphonse Vien, *Le Bon Ton*, 1843. By permission of the Mary Evans Picture Library.

39: A Victorian woman preparing for her bath. This photograph, taken c.1890s, represents some of the most daring public photography of the time. Bettmann / CORBIS.

40: James Herbert Draper, *Ulysses and the Sirens*, 1909. Oil on canvas. Ferens Art Gallery, Hull City Museums and Art Galleries, UK. By permission of the Bridgeman Art Library.

41: Frederic Leighton, *The Fisherman and the Syren: From a Ballad by Goethe*, c.1856–8. Oil on canvas. Bristol City Museum and Art Gallery, UK. By permission of the Bridgeman Art Library. Highly detailed and erotically charged, this famous painting by Leighton (1830–1896) and the one by Herbert Draper on the previous page explore the *femme fatale* theme that nineteenth-century English artists found so compelling. According to Greek myth, the sirens lured mariners to their deaths with their irresistible song. Ulysses, warned of their danger by the witch Circe, stopped the ears of his comrades with beeswax, then had himself bound to the mast of his ship so that he could hear the sweet music without succumbing to its treacherous spell.

42: (left and right) Earth Erotica by Heather Firth. Firth's extraordinary images, developed without specialized filters or digital enhancement, celebrate the inherent beauty, creative power and spiritual essence of sexuality as expressed in the landscape. (Middle) Seeds in milkweed pod. Karen Tweedy-Holmes / CORBIS.

43: Interior corridor within the Cave of the Cumaean Sybil, Italy. Mimmo Jodice / CORBIS.

44: Three of the dinner plates featured in artist Judy Chicago's groundbreaking art installation *The Dinner Party* — (from left to right) *Primordial Goddess*, *Sappho* and *Marcella*. By permission of Judy Chicago.

45: Nicola Tree / Getty Images.

46: (top) This illustration is one of many period drawings and engravings from eighteenth- and nineteenth-century France featured in *French Eroticism: The Joy of Life* by Piero Lorenzoni and Gabriele Mandel. By permission of Gabriele Mandel. (Bottom) Pen-and-ink drawings of vulvas. By permission of Betty Dodson.

48: (top) René Magritte, *Le Viol*, 1934. Oil on canvas. Menil Collection, Houston, Texas. By permission of the Bridgeman Art Library. Surrealist painter René Magritte (1898–1967), whose artistic signature was putting familiar objects in bizarre juxtaposition, succeeded brilliantly with this disturbing, yet also amusing, work (translated in English as *The Rape*). When the image was first unveiled in 1934, it was considered so scandalous that it was hung in a private room for selected viewing. (Bottom) Siede Preis / Getty Images.

Chapter Two

50: Lightscapes Photography, Inc. / CORBIS.

52: Leland Bobbé / CORBIS.

54: Standing female torso, probably Nefertiti, wife of Pharoah Amenophis IV Akhenaton, or an Amarnian princess. Quartzite, Egyptian, New Kingdom, 18th Dynasty, c.1365–1349 B.C. Louvre, Paris, France. Photo: Hervé Lewandowski. By permission of Réunion des Musées Nationaux / Art Resource, NY.

55: (left) Sophia Loren in a scene from *Marriage Italian Style*. Photographed on location in Rome, 1964. Bettmann / CORBIS. (Right) By permission of Carol Beckwith and Angela Fisher / Robert Estall Agency, UK.

56: (top) Kitagawa Utamaro, *Woman Putting On Makeup*. Woodblock print. Musée Guimet, Paris, France. By permission of the Bridgeman Art Library. While the models for Kitagawa Utamaro's (1753–1806) portraits may have come from the streets and pleasure districts of the city, his depiction of them was highly idealized. And his signature style remains recognizable today — extremely tall and slender bodies, long necks, small shoulders and eyes and mouths that are no more than tiny slits. (Bottom) A sixteenth-century portrait (artist unknown) of Queen Elizabeth I in her coronation robes. Fine Art Photographic Library / CORBIS.

57: Charles William Mitchell, *Hypatia*, 1889. Laing Art Gallery, Newcastle upon Tyne (Tyne & Wear Museums). By permission of the Tyne & Wear Museums. This romanticized interpretation of the ancient story of Hypatia was Victorian artist Charles William Mitchell's (1854–1903) one spectacular success. Victorian audiences were already familiar with the tragedy, having read Charles Kingsley's romantic novel *Hypatia*. Mitchell chose for his work the dramatic moment when the pagan philosopher Hypatia, stripped and dragged to the church altar by a mob of fanatical monks, clasps her long golden locks to her naked body and appeals for justice and mercy. Interestingly, both Mitchell and Kingsley depict Hypatia as a young woman. In reality, she was in her sixties when she was brutally stoned to death by the frenzied mob.

58: Royalty-Free / CORBIS.

59: Reza Estakhrian / Getty Images.

60: Francesco Gessi (1588–1649), *Cupid Sharpening His Arrows*. Christie's Images, London, UK. By permission of the Bridgeman Art Library.

61: Annie Louisa Swynnerton, *Cupid and Psyche*, 1890. Oldham Art Gallery, Lancashire, UK. By permission of the Bridgeman Art Library. Annie Swynnerton (1844–1933) created most of her works in Italy, where she lived after her marriage to sculptor Joseph Swynnerton. Her style, clearly reminiscent of Renaissance painting, won her many admirers, including John Singer Sargent and Sir George Clausen.

62: Decorative atomizer. Undated engraving. Bettmann / CORBIS.

63: (top) Cinnamon bun. Susan Marie Anderson / Getty Images; (bottom) Lavender. Royalty-Free / CORBIS.

65: (top, from left to right) White asparagus. Royalty-Free / CORBIS; Pomegranate. CORBIS; Emerging may apple in mid-April. Joe McDonald / CORBIS. (Bottom) Alexandre Cabanel, *The Birth of Venus*, 1863. Musée d'Orsay, Paris, France. By permission of Archivo Iconografico, SA / CORBIS. Influential academic painter Alexandre Cabanel (1823–1889), celebrated for the voluptuousness of his nudes, was one of many artists who brought the birth of Venus to life on canvas.

66: The chambered nautilus is a living fossil that has remained unchanged for over 400 million years. George B. Diebold / CORBIS.

67: Kim Cattrall, oyster in hand, on a beach in Cyprus — birthplace of the goddess Aphrodite. Excerpted from the documentary *Kim Cattrall: Sexual Intelligence*.

Chapter Three

68: Frederic Leighton, *The Bath of Psyche*, 1890. Oil on canvas. By permission of the Tate Gallery, London, UK / Art Resource, NY. Leighton, like many of his contemporaries, was influenced by a number of classical sculptures that set the standard for artistic creation at the time. He based the pose of Psyche on the ancient statue *Venus Leaving the Bath* that he had seen in Naples in 1859.

70: Sandro Botticelli, *The Birth of Venus*, c.1485. Tempera on canvas. Galleria degli Uffizi, Florence, Italy. Photograph by Summerfield Press. CORBIS. Botticelli's (1445–1510) painting is among the most famous rendering of this mythological moment — and certainly the most reproduced. It was commissioned by the Medici family and typifies the Renaissance preoccupation with classical mythology as a way of recapturing the former glory of Rome.

71: (bottom) Marilyn Monroe lying in the surf, c.1950–3. Underwood & Underwood / CORBIS; (inset, left) Bo Derek, from the film *10*. CP / Everett Collection; (inset, right) Halle Berry, from the film *Die Another Day*. CP / Everett Collection.

72: Guillaume Seignac, *The Water Nymph*. Whitford & Hughs, London, UK. By permission of the Bridgeman Art Library. Reproduced on countless posters and postcards, French painter Guillaume Seignac's (1870–1924) lush works are still appreciated today, as much for their delightful play of eroticism and light as for their classical imagery.

74: Agnolo Bronzino, *An Allegory with Venus and Cupid*, c.1540–50. Oil on panel. National Gallery, London, UK. By permission of the Bridgeman Art Library. Agnolo Bronzino (1503–1572) was the leading court painter of the

Florentine School in the middle of the sixteenth century. His allegories are recognizable for their seductive nudes posed against a backdrop of symbolic figures and luxurious fabric.

76: Woman kissing baby's head. Barnaby Hall / Photonica.

77: (left) Ancient Roman sculpture, torso of man. Mimmo Jodice / CORBIS; (right) Excerpted from the documentary *Kim Cattrall: Sexual Intelligence*.

78: Rick Gomez / CORBIS.

81: Heart maze created by Christopher Zacharow. Images.com / CORBIS.

82: Tim Pannell / CORBIS.

83: Tom & Dee Ann McCarthy / CORBIS.

85: Edward Holub. Taxi / Getty Images.

86: Origami vulva. Animation by Laura Sheppard and Sam Javanrouh. Courtesy of Optix Digital Pictures, Toronto. Excerpted from the documentary *Kim Cattrall: Sexual Intelligence.*

Chapter Four

89: Evelyn De Morgan, *Cadmus and Harmonia*, 1877. Oil on canvas. The De Morgan Centre for the Study of Nineteenth-Century Art and Society, London, UK. By permission of the Bridgeman Art Library. According to legend, the ancient Greek hero Cadmus married the beautiful Harmonia (daughter of Aphrodite and Mars) but was later transformed into a snake by the angry gods. The first moments after his transformation are captured poignantly by Evelyn De Morgan (1855–1919), who undoubtedly was inspired by these lines from Ovid's *Metamorphoses*: "With lambent tongue he kissed her patient face / Crept in her bosom as his dwelling place. / Entwined her neck, and shared the loved embrace."

90–91: Animation by Mike Brown, Sam Javanrouh and Ryan V. Hays. Courtesy of Optix Digital Pictures, Toronto. Excerpted from the documentary *Kim Cattrall: Sexual Intelligence.*

92: Bartolomeo Ammannati, *Leda and the Swan*. Marble. Bargello, Florence, Italy. By permission of the Bridgeman Art Library.

93: Gustav Klimt, *Danae*, 1907–08. Oil on canvas. Private Collection. By permission of the Bridgeman Art Library. Although the name of Austrian artist Gustav Klimt (1862–1918) is synonymous today with beautiful and sensual works of art, uniquely rendered, he was a controversial figure during his lifetime — and his paintings were constantly criticized for being too erotic, his symbolism too deviant.

94: Arthur Hacker, T*he Cloud*, 1902. Bradford Art Galleries and Museums, West Yorkshire, UK. By permission of The Bridgeman Art Library / Getty Images. Lisa J. Curtis, who reviewed the exhibition, *Exposed: The Victorian Nude*, at the Brooklyn Museum of Art in 2002, said of Arthur Hacker's (1858–1919) nude dream fantasy: "It seems as if Hacker snatched the white tufts [of cloud] right from the blue sky and employed them in this painting. It is so ethereal it doesn't seem as though it could come from paint and a brush."

95: Two women making love. Barnaby Hall / Photonica.

96: Salvador Dalí, *One Second before Awakening from a Dream, Caused by the Flight of a Bee around a Pomegranate*, 1944. Oil on canvas. © Salvador Dalí. Fundació Gala–Salvador Dalí / VEGAP (Madrid) / SODRAC (Montreal) 2005. Art Resource, NY. A master of fantasy, Salvador Dalí (1904–1989) brought to life on canvas a violent yet erotic dream that his muse and lover (later his wife) Gala Eluard described to him while

they were living in America. Dalí later commented that this was the first illustration of Freud's discovery that external stimuli could be the cause of a dream.

98: Torso of woman in corset. Lisa Powers / Photonica.

99: (left) Tamara de Lempicka, *The Slave*, 1927–29. Oil on canvas. Private Collection. © Estate of Tamara de Lempicka / ADAGP (Paris) / SODRAC (Montreal) 2005. Art Resource, NY. Polish-American artist Tamara de Lempicka (1898–1980), an Art Deco icon, perfected an original style that remains her signature to this day. She painted at a time when there was real excitement (and concern) about the impact of modernity on women's lives. Her figures adopt their formal poses against a changing world shaped by revolution, social aspiration, the Great Depression and the radicalization of European politics. (Middle) James Martin, Stone / Getty Images; (right) Ajamu / Photonica.

100: (top) Excerpted from the documentary *Kim Cattrall: Sexual Intelligence*; (bottom) Royalty-Free. Brand-X Pictures / Getty Images.

101: Steve Prezant / CORBIS.

103: Period drawing from *French Eroticism: The Joy of Life* by Piero Lorenzoni and Gabriele Mandel. By permission of Gabriele Mandel.

104: Debra McClinton, The Image Bank / Getty Images.

105: D.E.H. / Photonica.

106: Ondrea Barbe / CORBIS.

107: LWA-Dann Tardif / CORBIS.

108: (left) Gypsy Rose Lee. Underwood & Underwood / CORBIS; (right) Lili St. Cyr, c.1954. John Springer Collection / CORBIS.

109: (left) Josephine Baker, c.1920s. Bettmann / CORBIS; (right) Mae West, from the film *The Heat's On*. Bettmann / CORBIS.

110: *The Callipige Aphrodite*, from the Farnese Collection, 2nd Century B.C. Marble. Museo Archeologico Nazionale, Naples, Italy. By permission of the Bridgeman Art Library.

111: (left) Brigitte Bardot, c.1960s. Underwood & Underwood / CORBIS; (right) Marilyn Monroe, during publicity for the film *The Seven Year Itch*. Getty Images.

112: (top left) Dress of beads. From the Petrie Museum of Egyptian Archaeology, University College London, UK. (Middle) Model wearing paillette minidress, 1966. Photograph by David McCabe. Condé Nast Archive / CORBIS. (Right) Model wearing clear plastic dress decorated with sequins, by designer Paco Rabanne, 1991. Julio Donoso / CORBIS SYGMA. (Bottom) Dancers. Ian Sanderson / Photonica.

113: (far left) Hubert de la Tour / CORBIS; (top left) A dancer at Le Lido, Paris, France, 2004. Maher Attar / CORBIS; (top right) Woman at window. Photonica; (bottom) Bubble dancer Sally Rand, c.1930s. Bettmann / CORBIS.

115: Photograph by Michael Halsband.

Chapter Five

116: Salvador Dalí, *Meditative Rose*, 1958. Mr. and Mrs. Arnold Grant Collection, New York. © Salvador Dalí. Fundació Gala–Salvador Dalí / VEGAP (Madrid) / SODRAC (Montreal) 2005. Dalí used roses in his works as a female sexual symbol. Note the tiny drop of water on one of the petals of the flower, as realistic as a photograph. Dalí often employed the *trompe l'oeil* effect to highlight a small detail within a painting.

119: *Barberini Faun*. Roman copy after Hellenistic original, c.220 B.C.E. Marble. Glyptothek, Staatliche Antikensammlungen, Munich, Germany. Vanni / Art Resource, NY. Freestanding and larger than life, this erotically charged sculpture, also known as the *Sleeping Satyr*, is a celebration of the male figure in languid repose.

120: Royalty-Free / Getty Images.

121: Vassily Kandinsky, *Color Studies with Technical Explanations* (detail). © Estate of Vassily Kandinsky / ADAGP (Paris) / SODRAC (Montreal) 2005.

122: (top) Michael Gesinger / Photonica; (bottom) Kaliste / CORBIS.

123: (top left) William Manning / CORBIS; (top right) Mark Hill / Photonica; (bottom) Royalty-Free / CORBIS.

124: Excerpted from the documentary *Kim Cattrall: Sexual Intelligence*.

125: Simeon Solomon, *Love in Autumn*, 1866. Private Collection. By permission of the owner. Like so many artists in his circle, Solomon (1840–1905) found himself attracted to pagan and classical themes. But the real subject of this painting is one to which he often returned — the vulnerability of love. Solomon's contribution to the artistic community extends beyond his paintings, for he chose to live openly as a homosexual at a time when it was not socially acceptable to do so. In 1873, his career and his life collapsed when he was arrested for homosexual offences. Unable, or perhaps unwilling, to return to respectable society, he became a vagabond and alcoholic but continued to paint and draw.

126: Antonio Canova, *Psyche Revived by the Kiss of Love* (detail). Marble. Louvre, Paris, France. By permission of the Bridgeman Art Library. Italian Antonio Canova (1757–1822), a prolific sculptor, seduced the whole of Europe with his mythological compositions — a purity of contours shaping a discrete eroticism. *Psyche Revived by the Kiss of Love* entered the Louvre in 1824.

127: A crescent sliver of Earth, photographed by the crew of *Apollo 12*. NASA / Roger Ressmeyer / CORBIS.

129: Thomas Alexander Harrison, *In Arcadia*. Oil on canvas. Musée d'Orsay, Paris. Photo: Hervé Lewandowski. By permission of Réunion des Musées Nationaux / Art Resource, NY. According to Barbara Dayer Gallati, curator of American Art at the Brooklyn Museum of Art, "Harrison's (1855–1930) *In Arcadia* was unveiled to high praise at the Paris Salon of 1886, where French critics appreciated its naturalistic vision of the female nude that merged academic subject matter with progressive plein-air painting techniques. The title was probably chosen to distance the robust women from the here-and-now by placing them in an imaginary, nostalgic sphere."

131: Dutch photographer Margriet Smulders, *Les Fleurs du Mal*, 2002.

132: Lester Lefkowitz / CORBIS.

134–135: Excerpted from the documentary *Kim Cattrall: Sexual Intelligence*.

All excerpts from the documentary *Kim Cattrall: Sexual Intelligence*: Kim Cattrall, Executive Producer; Catherine Annau, Director; Amanda Enright, Producer; Jeffrey Kindley, Richard L. Green, Amy Briamonte, Writers; Stefan von Bjorn, Principal Director of Photography; Michael Grippo, Director of Photography. Copyright Sexual Intelligence Inc. 2005.

Index

A
Abbas Giant, 27–28
Abramson, Paul, 51
An Allegory on Venus and Cupid (Bronzino), 74
Allende, Isabel, 64
Ammannati, Bartolomeo, 95
Angier, Natalie, 48–49
Antony (interviewee), 13, 14, 19, 35, 47, 79, 118
aphrodisiacs, 63–67
Aphrodite, 30, 64, 70–75, 108, 124
Aphrodite (Allende), 64
Augustine, St., 31

B
Bader, Michael, 17, 49, 51, 69, 75, 93–95, 100, 102, 104
Baker, Josephine, 109
Bartles, Andreas, 80
Baumeister, Roy, 15
Beckwith, Carol, 59
Bentley, Eric, 74
The Book of the Penis (Paley), 21, 92
brain, as sexual organ, 15, 51–67, 80
Braun, Virginia, 20
Brillat-Savarin, Jean Anthelme, 64
Bronzino, Agnolo, 74
Buston, Peter, 83

C
Carson, Anne, 126
Cayra (interviewee), 17, 19, 47, 88, 95, 104, 126
Chicago, Judy, 44
Clarke, John R., 28–30, 107
clitoris, 48–49
Crenshaw, Theresa, 75
"cuddle chemicals," 83
Cupid, 60

D
"divided monster," 38, 40
Dodson, Betty, 20, 34, 36–37, 46–49, 66, 102
domination fantasies, 91, 102

E
ears, 58–59
Emlen, Stephen, 83
erections, 21–22
Eros, 60, 124
erotic art, 32, 33, 44–47, 74, 93
Etcoff, Nancy, 34–35, 53
experimentation, 114, 117
eye contact, 53

F
fantasy, 88–115
fascinum, 30
fashions, 38–41, 58–59, 100–1
female sexual dysfunction, 15
fetishes, 22, 98–101
Fisher, Angela, 59
Fisher, Helen, 53, 80–83
foods, 64–67
fragrances, 62–64

G
Gemmell, Nikki, 17
A General Theory of Love, 83
genitalia, 19–49
slang names for, 19–21
Gräfenberg, Ernst, 48
Graham, Cynthia, 16
Greeks, sexual attitudes, 33, 126
G spot, 48–49

H
hair, 56–58, 77
Hansbury, Griffin, 21–22
heart, 122–23
Hirsch, Alan R., 63
Hollander, Anne, 38, 40, 56–58

Honoring the Sensual Self (Steinberg), 83
hormones, 60, 80
humor, 104–108

I
imprinting, 75–76
intimacy, 124–8

J
Jacoby, Alexandra, 47
Johnson, Virginia E., 34

K
Keen, Sam, 128
Kiisti (interviewee), 14, 17, 35, 48, 51, 77, 117, 118, 126
kissing, 78–79
Kitzinger, Celia, 20

L
laughter, 104–108
Leda, 92
Lee, Gypsy Rose, 112
Liberating Masturbation (Dodson), 46–47
Lisa (interviewee), 14, 19, 20, 35, 48, 62, 77, 117, 128, 130
Loren, Sophia, 59
love
ancients' view of, 86
and sex, 118, 128–30
triggered by lust, 80
Love in the Time of Cholera (Marquez), 53
love map, 75–76

M
Maltz, Wendy, 36, 93, 95, 102, 107
Márquez, Gabriel Garcia, 53
marriage, 86
Mars, 124
Masters, William H., 34

masturbation, 46, 92–93
Mencken, H.L., 112
mermaids, 40
Miles, Christopher, 86, 89
Mohanraj, Mary Anne, 130
Money, John, 60, 75
Monick, Eugene, 28
Moore, Thomas, 13, 42, 58, 70–73, 79, 97, 108, 118, 126, 130
Morin, Jack, 114
mythology, 40, 60, 70–75, 93, 124

N
Narcissus, 75
Natasha (interviewee), 14, 19, 22, 35, 47, 69, 77, 97, 118
National Archaeological Museum of Naples, 31, 32–33
Norwich, John Julius, 86, 89

O
O'Keeffe, Georgia, 44
Onan, 93

P
Paley, Maggie, 21, 32, 92
Panati, Charles, 60, 100
penis, 19, 21, 23–25, 33–35
penis envy, 24–25
perfume, 62–64
personality traits, 83, 84
phalluses, 27–32, 107
pheromones, 62–64
physical traits, 77
Pinkerton, Steven, 51
Pompeii, 28, 30–31, 33, 89
pornography, 31, 48
power games, 114
Priapus, 30, 107
pubic hair, 48

R
Rado, James, 56
Ragni, Gerome, 56
Rätsch, Christian, 66
relationships, 83–84
repression, 128–30
Rilke, Rainer Maria, 120
ritual, 118–20
*The Rocky Horror
    Picture Show*, 112
Rodgers, Joann Ellison, 76, 107
Roland (interviewee), 14, 19,
    47, 88, 128
Romans, sexual attitudes,
    28–30, 34, 86
Roman Sex (Clarke), 28, 107
romantic attachment, 83–86

S
Saint-Exupéry, Antoine de, 84
Sappho, 13
scent, 62–64
Scentsational Sex (Hirsch), 63
"Secret Museum," 31–33
Seki, Semir, 80
self-knowledge, 83
Semans, Anne, 17
The Seven Year Itch, 60
Sex: A Natural History
    (Rodgers), 76, 107
Sex and Suits (Hollander),
    56–58
*Sexy Origins and Intimate
    Things* (Panati), 60, 100
shoes, 100–1
Sims, Michael, 54
The Soul of Sex (Moore), 13,
    58, 70

St. Cyr, Lily, 112
Steinberg, David, 83
Sternberg, Robert J., 76, 84
stiletto heel, 100–1
Stoller, Robert J., 53, 75
striptease, 108–13
Survival of the Prettiest (Etcoff),
    34–35, 53

T
taboos, 87–89, 112
Tannahill, Reay, 38
Tarik (interviewee), 14, 22, 35,
    69, 88, 118, 120
testosterone, 21–22
Thorton, Bruce, 124
Tristan and Isolde, 44

V
verbal communication, 17–18
Viagra, 15, 17
visual stimulation, 53
vulva, 36–48, 54

W
water, 70–73
West, Mae, 113
Why We Love (Helen Fisher),
    80–83
Winks, Cathy, 17
Wyatt, Tristram, 62

Z
Zeitlin, Froma, 74–75
Zeus, 93, 124

Selected Bibliography

Abramson, Paul R. and Steven D. Pinkerton.
*With Pleasure: Thoughts on the
Nature of Human Sexuality.*
New York: Oxford University Press, 1995.

Allen, Robert C.
*Horrible Prettiness: Burlesque and
American Culture.*
Chapel Hill, NC: University of North
Carolina Press, 1991.

Allende, Isabel.
Aphrodite: A Memoir of the Senses.
New York: HarperFlamingo, 1998.

Angier, Natalie.
Woman: An Intimate Geography.
New York: Anchor Books, 2000.

Anonymous (Nikki Gemmell).
The Bride Stripped Bare.
New York: Fourth Estate /
HarperCollins 2003.

Bader, Michael J.
*Arousal: The Secret Logic of
Sexual Fantasies.*
New York: St. Martin's Griffin, 2003.

Baumeister, R. "Erotic plasticity
and female sexuality." *Psychological
Bulletin* 126, 2000.

Beckwith, Carol and Angela Fisher.
African Ceremonies.
New York: Harry N. Abrams, 2002.

Bentley, Richard.
Erotic Art.
London: Quartet Books, 1984.

Blumberg, Eric S.
"The Lives and Voices of Highly Sexual
Women." *The Journal of Sex Research* 40,
no. 2, May 2003:146–157.

Braun, Virginia and Celia Kitzinger.
"'Snatch,' 'Hole,' or 'Honey-pot'?
Semantic Categories and the Problem of
Nonspecificity in Female Genital Slang."
The Journal of Sex Research 38, no. 2,
May 2001:146–158.

Brumberg, Joan Jacobs.
*The Body Project: An Intimate
History of American Girls.*
Vintage, 1998.

Buston, Peter M. and Stephen T. Emlen.
"Cognitive processes underlying human
mate choice: the relationship between
self-perception and mate preference in
Western society." *PNAS*, July 22, 2003.

Carson, Anne.
Eros the Bittersweet.
Normal, IL: Dalkey Archive Press, 1998.

Cattrall, Kim and Mark Levinson.
Satisfaction: The Art of the Female Orgasm.
New York: Warner Books, 2002.

Chevalier, Jean and Alain Gheerbrant.
The Penguin Dictionary of Symbols.
Penguin Books, 1997.

Chivers, Meredith L., Gerulf Rieger,
Elizabeth Latty, J. Michael Bailey.
"A Sex Difference in the Specificity of
Sexual Arousal." Northwestern University.
In press, *Psychological Science.*

Clark, Kenneth.
The Nude: A Study in Ideal Form.
Princeton, NJ: Princeton
University Press, 1972.

Clarke, John R.
Roman Sex.
New York: Harry N. Abrams, 2003.

Crenshaw, Theresa L.
*The Alchemy of Love and Lust:
Discovering Our Sex Hormones and How
They Determine Who We Love, When We
Love, and How Often We Love.*
New York: G.P. Putnam's Sons, 1996.

Dodson, Betty.
Liberating Masturbation.
Self-published.

_____. *Orgasms for Two:
The Joy of Partnersex.*
New York: Harmony Books, 2002.

_____. *Sex for One:
The Joy of Selfloving.*
New York: Three Rivers Press, 1996.

_____. "The Sounds and
Words of Sexual Pleasure."
www.bettydodson.com/soundsex.htm,
1997.

The Economist, February 12, 2004:
"The Science of Love:
I Get a Kick out of You."

Etcoff, Nancy.
*Survival of the Prettiest:
The Science of Beauty.*
New York: Doubleday, 1999.

Fisher, Helen.
Anatomy of Love.
New York: Ballantine Books, 1994.

_____. *Why We Love: The
Nature and Chemistry of Romantic Love.*
New York: Henry Holt, 2004.

Foucault, Michel.
The History of Sexuality: An Introduction.
Vintage, 1990.

Friday, Nancy.
*Women on Top: How Real Life Has
Changed Women's Sexual Fantasies.*
New York: Pocket Books, 1991.

Gates, Katharine.
Deviant Desires: Incredibly Strange Sex.
Juno Books, 2000.

Gilbert, Harriett, ed.
The Sexual Imagination from Acker to Zola.
London: Jonathan Cape, 1993.

Graham, Cynthia et al.
"Turning On and Turning Off: A Focus
Group Study of the Factors That Affect
Women's Sexual Arousal,"
Archives of Sexual Behavior 33, no. 6,
December 2004.

Hansbury, Griffin.
"Sexual TNT: A transman tells the truth
about testosterone." *Journal of Gay and
Lesbian Psychotherapy.* Vol. 8 no. 1/2,
2004, pp. 7–18.

Hersey, George L.
*The Evolution of Allure: Sexual
Selection from the Medici Venus
to the Incredible Hulk.*
Cambridge, MA: The MIT Press, 1996.

Hicks, Thomas V. and Harold Leitenberg.
"Sexual Fantasies about One's Partner
Versus Someone Else." *The Journal of
Sex Research* 38, no. 1,
February 2001: 43–50.

Hirsch, Alan R.
*Scentsational Sex: The Secret to
Using Aroma for Arousal.*
Boston, Mass.: Element Books, 1998.

Hollander, Anne.
Seeing through Clothes.
Berkeley, CA: University of
California Press, 1993.

_____. *Sex and Suits: The Evolution of
Modern Dress.* Kodansha Globe, 1995.

Hyde, Janet Shibley, John D. DeLamater,
E. Sandra Byers.
Understanding Human Sexuality.
Toronto: McGraw-Hill Ryerson, 2004.

Jackson, William T.H.
*The Anatomy of Love: The Tristan
of Gottfried Von Strassburg.*
New York: Columbia University
Press, 1971.

Johnson, Catherine, Betsey Stirratt
and John Bancroft, ed.
*Sex and Humor: Selections from
The Kinsey Institute.*
Bloomington: Indiana University
Press, 2002.

Keen, Sam.
To Love and Be Loved.
New York: Bantam Books, 1997.

www.kinseyinstitute.org

Kohl, James Vaughn and Robert T.
Francoeur.
*The Scent of Eros: Mysteries of
Odor in Human Sexuality.*
New York: Continuum, 1995.

Lewis, Thomas, Fari Amini
and Richard Lannon.
A General Theory of Love.
New York: Random House, 2000.

Lucie-Smith, Edward.
Symbolist Art.
London: Thames & Hudson, 1985.

Maltz, Wendy and Suzie Boss.
*Private Thoughts: Exploring the
Power of Women's Sexual Fantasies.*
Novato, California: New World
Library, 2001.

Miles, Christopher and
John Julius Norwich.
Love in the Ancient World.
New York: Sterling Publishing, 2000.

Mohanraj, Mary Anne (ed.).
*Aqua Erotica: Eighteen Stories
for a Steamy Bath.*
New York: Three Rivers Press, 2000.

Money, John.
*Lovemaps: Clinical Concepts of
Sexual/Erotic Health and Pathology,
Paraphilia, and Gender Transposition in
Childhood, Adolescence, and Maturity.*
New York: Prometheus Books, 1988.

Monick, Eugene.
Phallos: Sacred Image of the Masculine.
Toronto: Inner City Books, 1987.

Moore, Thomas.
*The Soul of Sex: Cultivating Life
as an Act of Love.*
New York: HarperCollins, 1998.

Morin, Jack.
The Erotic Mind.
New York: HarperCollins, 1995.

Paglia, Camille.
Sex, Art and American Culture.
Vintage, 1992.

_____. *Sexual Personae:
Art & Decadence from Nefertiti to
Emily Dickinson.*
Vintage, 1991.

Paley, Maggie.
The Book of the Penis.
New York: Grove Press, 1999.

Panati, Charles.
*Sexy Origins and Intimate Things:
The Rites and Rituals of Straights, Gays,
Bi'S, Drags, Trans, Virgins and Others.*
Penguin Books, 1998.

Rätsch, Christian.
*Plants of Love: Aphrodisiacs in History
and a Guide to Their Identification.*
Berkeley, CA: Ten Speed Press, 1997.

Rodgers, Joann Ellison.
Sex: A Natural History.
New York: Times Books, 2001.

Sims, Michael.
*Adam's Navel: A Natural and Cultural
History of the Human Form.*
Viking Press, 2003.

Smith, Alison, ed.
Exposed: The Victorian Nude.
New York: Watson-Guptill
Publications, 2002.

Sohn, Amy.
Sex and the City: Kiss and Tell.
New York: Melcher Media/Pocket
Books, 2004.

Steinberg, David, ed.
*The Erotic Impulse: Honoring
the Sensual Self.*
New York: Jeremy P. Tarcher/Perigee,
1992.

Sternberg, Robert J.
*Love Is a Story: A New Theory
of Relationships.*
New York: Oxford University Press, 1998.

Stoller, Robert J.
Observing the Erotic Imagination.
New Haven, CT: Yale University
Press, 1985.

Tannahill, Reay.
Sex in History.
Chelsea, MI: Scarborough House, 1992.

Thorton, Bruce.
Eros: The Myth of Ancient Greek Sexuality.
Boulder, CO: Westview Press, 1998.

Tiefer, Leonore.
Sex is Not a Natural Act and Other Essays.
Boulder, CO: Westview Press, 1995.

Varone, Antonio.
Eroticism in Pompeii.
Los Angeles, CA: J. Paul Getty Trust
Publications, 2001.

Winks, Cathy and Anne Semans.
The Good Vibrations Guide to Sex. 3rd ed.
San Francisco: Cleis Press, 2002.

Wyatt, Tristan D.
*Pheromones and Animal Behaviour:
Communication by Smell and Taste.*
Cambridge: Cambridge University
Press, 2003.

Zeitlin, Froma I.
*Playing the Other: Gender and Society
in Classical Greek Literature*
(Women in Culture and Society Series).
Chicago: University of Chicago Press, 1995.

Zilbergeld, Bernie.
The New Male Sexuality. Rev. ed.
New York: Bantam Books, 1999.

The publisher would like to acknowledge, with enormous thanks, the following people for their invaluable help, unflagging enthusiasm, generosity and grace during the making of this book:

Kim Cattrall, who gave us this wonderful opportunity to work with her on one of her most ambitious projects yet.

Amy Briamonte, whose sheer force of vision (plus her capacity to never sleep or to stray far from her cellphone) moved *Sexual Intelligence* from first draft to inspired book.

Gord Sibley, for brilliant design above and beyond the call — and for one of the most beautiful jackets Madison has ever produced. Special thanks to photographer Wayne Maser, for so generously providing his image of Kim Cattrall for the front cover (and to Ken Davis, for coming to our rescue with such speed and grace!).

At Fertile Ground Productions, producer Amanda Enright and her colleagues Leah Temerty and Rachael Rotsaert. Your encouragement and your ready help with all questions large and small added much ease to this collaborative adventure.

At Optix Digital Pictures, Subi Vaid and Sam Javanrouh. You set new records for "turnaround time!" Many thanks for always answering our call....

Editorial Director
Wanda Nowakowska

Book Design
Gordon Sibley

Project Editor
Anna Cundari

Photo Research
Anna Cundari
Bao-Nghi Nhan

Vice President, Business Affairs and Production
Susan Barrable

Production Manager
Donna Chong

Printed by
Imago Productions (F.E.) Ltd.,
Singapore

Kim Cattrall
sexualintelligence

was produced by
Madison Press Books